"Jeanette Howard has laboured in ministry dealing with sexuality for decades, and is well qualified to speak to the current issues and ministry challenges involved. To read *Dwelling in the Land* is to soak in reasoned, clear, biblically based principles, lessons learned from a woman who's been there, done that, and is doing it well."

Joe Dallas, author and pastoral counsellor

Jeanette Howard is the Director of Bethany Life Ministries in the UK. While living in California back in the late 1980s Jeanette began to address a number of personal issues, including gender dysphoria, same-sex attraction, and familial relationship problems, bringing each area into the light and truth of the Bible. For many years Jeanette has spoken and ministered in this difficult area. She is author of *Out of Egypt* and *Into the Promised Land*.

Dwelling in the Land

Bringing same-sex attraction under
the Lordship of Christ

Jeanette Howard

MONARCH
BOOKS

Oxford UK, and Grand Rapids, USA

Published by Monarch Books
an imprint of
Lion Hudson plc
Wilkinson House, Jordan Hill Road,
Oxford OX2 8DR, England
Email: monarch@lionhudson.com
www.lionhudson.com/monarch

ISBN 978 0 85721 623 6
e-ISBN 978 0 85721 624 3

First edition 2015

Acknowledgments
Unless otherwise noted, Scripture quotations taken from the Holy Bible, New International Version, copyright © 1973, 1978, 1984 International Bible Society. Used by permission of Hodder & Stoughton, a member of the Hodder Headline Group. All rights reserved. "NIV" is a trademark of International Bible Society. UK trademark number 1448790.
Scripture quotations marked "AMP" are taken from the Amplified® Bible, Copyright © 1954, 1958, 1962, 1965, 1987 by The Lockman Foundation. Used by permission.
Scripture quotations marked "J. B. Phillips" are taken from *The New Testament in Modern English*, Revised Edition, translated by J. B. Phillips. Copyright © 1958, 1960, 1972 by J. B. Phillips. Reprinted with permission of Simon & Schuster.
Scripture quotations marked "KJV" are taken from The Authorized (King James) Version. Rights in the Authorized Version are vested in the Crown. Reproduced by permission of the Crown's patentee, Cambridge University Press.
Scripture quotations marked "NASB" are taken from the New American Standard Bible®, Copyright © 1960, 1962, 1963, 1968, 1971, 1972, 1973, 1975, 1977, 1995 by The Lockman Foundation. Used by permission.
Scripture quotations marked "NCV" are taken from the New Century Version. Copyright © by Thomas Nelson, Inc. Used by permission. All rights reserved.
Scripture quotations marked "NLT" are taken from the *Holy Bible, New Living Translation*, copyright © 1996, 2004, 2007 by Tyndale House Foundation. Used by permission of Tyndale House Publishers, Inc., Carol Stream, Illinois 60188. All rights reserved.
Scripture quotations marked "The Message" are taken from *The Message*. Copyright © by Eugene H. Peterson 1993, 1994, 1995, 1996, 2000, 2001, 2002. Used by permission of NavPress Publishing Group.
Scripture quotations marked "NKJV" are taken from the New King James Version. Copyright © 1982 by Thomas Nelson, Inc. Used by permission. All right reserved.
Extracts pp. 34, 43, 44–45 taken from *Understanding Sexual Identity: A Resource for Youth Ministry* by Mark A. Yarhouse © 2013 by Mark A. Yarhouse. Used by permission of Zondervan. www.zondervan.com
Extract pp. 39–40 taken from "The Three Tier Distinction" by Mark A. Yarhouse, http://www.sexualidentityinstitute.org/archives/13237. Used by permission.
Extract pp. 64–65 taken from *Washed and Waiting: Reflections on Christian Faithfulness and Homosexuality* by Wesley Hill © 2010 by Wesley Hill. Used by permission of Zondervan. www.zondervan.com
Extract p. 68 taken from "You and Me Together" by Peter Ould © 19 April 2007, Peter Ould. An Exercise in the Fundamentals of Orthodoxy: Blog Available from: www.peter-ould.net/2007/04/19/you-and-me-together. Used by permission.
Extract p. 262 taken from *Gold Cord: The Story of a Fellowship* by Amy Carmichael, © 1932 by The Dohnavur Fellowship. Used by permission of CLC Publications. May not be further reproduced. All rights reserved.
Maps pp. 116, 227, 228 © Lion Hudson/Tim Dowley Associates Ltd.

A catalogue record for this book is available from the British Library

Printed and bound in the UK, September 2015, LH26

Contents

SECTION 4

How we view God and understand His sovereignty will determine our readiness to obey, irrespective of how we feel. Our attitude towards Him determines the potential depth of our relationship with Him.

SECTION 5

The "land" we have been allocated may not be what we had hoped for, but it is still our inheritance. If it is flat and fertile, then we plant crops. And if it is rugged and hilly, we shepherd sheep. It is what we make it.

Dwelling in the Land *is dedicated to my friend Tony Ives who sat on the Bethany Life Ministries Board of Trustees. It was his hard work and dedication that enabled the ministry to be built on a sure foundation and later obtain charitable status.*

But he was so much more. Primarily, Tony was my friend who loved, supported, and encouraged me at all times and in so many ways. Both he and his wife Pam opened their house to me so often that the guest room was known as Jeanette's room! They let me treat their garden as my own and, over the years, Tony learned to see it as a colourful expression of our multi-faceted Father and enjoy it in all its seasonal beauty.

Much of the first draft of Dwelling *was written whilst sitting in Jeanette's Room overlooking my garden. Thank you, my friend.*

Acknowledgments

This book would never have arrived at the point of publication without support and help from: The Bethany Life Ministries Board of Trustees; the ongoing financial support given generously by those who believe in me and the message God chooses to convey through my writing and speaking; Living Stones Community Church (especially the members of my Life Group); numerous friends who have intentionally been there for me both in person and/or through the social media; and Brad Sargent, who is not only a dear friend but is also capable of turning my creative expression into real sentences: a true hero to all who know him.

The following people have not only graciously allowed me to share parts of their story within the Dwelling narrative, but they have also read the first draft of the manuscript and were able to offer invaluable suggestions resulting in what you have before you. They are: Meleah Allard, Sonia Balcer, Phil Barnett, Nathan Collins, Carla Harshman, and Bob Ragan.

I also want to thank Tony Collins and Jessica Scott at Monarch Books for their behind-the-scene efforts.

Finally, based on the principle that the last shall be first, I want to thank our awesome triune God for His unrelenting love, acceptance, and enabling. I cannot manage a day without You and for that I am eternally grateful.

Introduction

In today's world the subject of homosexuality is rarely out of the headlines. No longer fearful of social or financial backlash, sports and film stars seem to be leaping out of the closet with reckless abandon on a near daily basis. Far from being ostracized by society, these men and women are now positively embraced as standard-bearers of a new, enlightened, and totally accepting civilization that is non-judgmental and all-inclusive. Any stance or voice that challenges this juggernaut of positivity is decried, decreed homophobic, and dismissed as being a relic from a bygone age of bigotry and hate.

The worldview is one thing, but when I consider homosexuality in light of Scripture I can certainly empathize with Winnie-the-Pooh when he states: "When you are a Bear of Very Little Brain, and you Think of Things, you find sometimes that a Thing which seemed very Thingish inside you is quite different when it gets out into the open and has other people looking at it."[1]

Although I personally find the biblical stance on active sexuality, of any gender combination, crystal clear, the Christian voice on the subject of homosexuality has rarely been more divided. Unfortunately, many of the discussions between the various factions appear to be little more than biblical hand grenades tossed at one another from the safety of a well-dug trench. Sadly, many of these dialogues often create more heat than light. However, even though I don't feel at all inclined or equipped to engage in such discussions, I certainly appreciate

1   A. A. Milne, *The House at Pooh Corner*, London: Methuen and Co. Ltd, 1928.

the fact that there is a conversation to be had and, thankfully, is being had by men and women from every facet of Christianity. From what I have read, it is clear that many are diligently seeking to "work out[their] salvation with fear and trembling" (Philippians 2:12). And for that persistence I salute them.

As with my first two books, *Out of Egypt* and *Into the Promised Land*, this book, *Dwelling in the Land*, is a result of my continued journey into, and toward, the things of God. I know the loneliness of growing up feeling "different" from everybody else. I know what it is like to live as a sexually active unbelieving gay woman. I know the agonizing choices that have to be made as a young believer committed to choosing God's ways over one's own desires. And I know what it is like to remain single for thirty years, still having to keep a watchful eye on some of the attractions and thoughts toward other women. This book is all about discipleship and the long haul. With contributions from men and women who have also walked faithfully and with sexual integrity for many years, this book is written to encourage fellow pilgrims to keep journeying along the right path.

Precisely because there is such a variety of thought within Christianity, perhaps before you start reading the first chapter, it may be helpful if I make my position completely clear. I have written this book based on the following criteria:

- I believe that one consequence of the Fall has been damage to our relationships with both men and women in all capacities of life, including the area of sexuality.
- While I acknowledge that some Christians hold differing beliefs, the book is written from the premise that the biblical pattern for sexual relationships is established in Genesis 2:24 and reinforced throughout the Bible.

- This means that I believe that all sexual activity (irrespective of orientation, attraction, or past behaviour) outside the boundaries of heterosexual marriage is not within God's plan for mankind, no matter how monogamous, faith-filled, and Christian-based it may be.
- I do not believe that a sexual relationship is essential for a meaningful life, and so I encourage all single Christians, whatever their orientation or attraction, to pursue a celibate life in deference to biblical truth.
- I wholeheartedly believe that our identity is found in Christ alone and that every believer, irrespective of attraction or situation, can enjoy a full, contented life in Him.

If, at any point, what you read seems to have veered away from those points above, then that inference will be due to a flaw in my writing skills rather than a fundamental change in my belief system! Now that you are conversant with my point of reference, it seems timely to look back to the late 1980s when my voyage of discovery began and note some of the changes that have occurred within society and the church during these past thirty years.

Section 1

Where have we been? Where are we now? And what is happening in Christendom?

Chapter 1

Post Exodus

Exodus International Conference
Loyola University
Los Angeles
Sunday, June 26th 1988

This morning I was woken by a 4.8 earthquake. It started with a bang followed by a swaying of the bed and a rattling of the wardrobe: an interesting way to wake up and start the conference.

Although my journal entry was brief and failed to comment on anything else that happened that day, my attendance at that 1988 meeting impacted my life and choices for years to come. It was the eighth Exodus International Conference, hosted by Andy Comiskey and Desert Stream Ministries, a ministry then based in Anaheim, California, USA. Living just north of San Francisco and being part of the women's residential programme run by Love in Action meant that I and a number of others from the ministry were able to drive the 350 or so miles south and attend this week-long event.

Judging from the notes I took, the main speaker that year was Dr John White, the eminent evangelical psychiatrist and author of such books as *Eros Defiled*, *Eros Redeemed*, and *Parents in Pain*. I had read his book *The Cost of Commitment* some three years earlier. That had been instrumental in convincing me, a non-believing homosexually active woman, that following Christ was costly but ultimately worthwhile. There were other well-known Exodus speakers teaching that year, including Sy Rogers, Alan Medinger, and of course Frank Worthen. Frank and his wife, Anita, had been influential in bringing me from the UK to the States in January of that year, and my time with the Love in Action ministry did much to deepen my relationship with the Lord.

FAQ: How long does it take to change from being a homosexual to being heterosexual?

Part of the ministry's brief at Love in Action was to visit churches, give presentations, and host a Q&A with the congregation. I was a young Christian, yet, despite all the relational difficulties and temptations I was facing, my hope was that eventually I would "come through" and be able to experience and enjoy love in a relationship acceptable to God. So when I heard Frank answer this frequently asked question with a gentle but confident "Five years seems to be the average time for someone to change", my heart soared.

All I needed to do, I concluded, was to pursue my relationship with Jesus and be obedient to all I read in the Bible. Then, as I thought and lived according to the Word and addressed certain issues in my life, I would gradually walk into and embrace a heterosexual identity, outlook, and attractions. It all seemed so logical and reasonable and godly. It was during this time in the States that I also had opportunity to sit in on several lectures given by the British research psychologist and theologian Dr Elizabeth Moberly as she expounded her theory concerning the root causes of homosexuality. Her book, *Homosexuality: A New Christian Ethic,*[2] had been published in 1983 and was embraced by the majority of those of us seeking to find a solution to our same-sex attraction (SSA).[3]

2   Elizabeth R. Moberly, *Homosexuality: A New Christian Ethic*, Cambridge: James Clarke & Co. Ltd, 1983.
3   Dr Moberly was one of the early proponents of the term known as "reparative therapy". She asserted that homosexual orientation does not derive from genetic, hormonal, or learned behaviour, but from a child's

In 1988 I was a young Christian who had hope for great change. Although my journal read like the script of a second-rate disaster movie, I was keen for Jesus to transform my life into something worthwhile. Despite lurching from one dependent relationship to the next, I was convinced, and encouraged to believe, that continual surrender to the ways of God would result in newness of life. *I still believe that to be true.* We are born again into the family of God, are citizens of another country, and live in a way that seeks to image Jesus Christ. But the newness of life that I had also hoped for and, in all honesty, back then in the 1980s had been led to believe *was probable rather than merely possible* – that of embracing a heterosexual mind set and way of life – never really materialized.

Having the right goal

Many will claim that a change in sexual orientation was never the goal of Exodus International and its affiliate ministries. Whether it was one of the organization's implicit goals or not, I can assure you that back in the 1980s the *expectation* of change was certainly fostered and encouraged. Dating and marriage were seen as very realistic goals and every wedding was celebrated as another example of healing and wholeness. If any

---

relationship with the same-sex parent early in life. Acknowledging that homosexual development is complex and multi-faceted, Moberly believed that there was a constant factor: a deficit in the relationship with the same-sex parent and a drive to make up for this deficit through same-sex relationships. Disruption in the attachment process, cites Moberly, can seriously hinder normal psychological and sexual development, and it is the drive to repair that damage, albeit subconsciously, that fuels the homosexual relationship. Therefore, Moberly concludes, learning to relate to members of one's own gender in a healthy non-dependent and non-defensive detachment way is key to addressing the homosexual drive. Further reading on this subject is readily available via the internet. Dr Moberly has now retired from conducting research on this subject and currently works in the field of cancer research.

of us did entertain questions over the suitability of some of the couples marrying, we certainly never voiced them in anything louder than a faint whisper. After all, we concluded, this was a continuum we were all walking along, and any difficulties that may arise could be addressed within the framework of marriage.

Thirty years on, we may well be accused of naivety by some people. But, at that time, it was certainly my genuine belief that I would gradually progress along the continuum from being fully homosexual in outlook to a much broader vision that not only valued, welcomed, and increasingly engaged with men, but also opened the door to heterosexual marriage. And this change would take place, I believed, as I kept addressing the problems I had with gender dysphoria – a strong feeling of not being the gender that I physically appeared to be, the attitudinal difficulties I held towards men and women, and my many other relational issues.

I am immensely grateful for the emphasis that was placed on Scripture during my time with Love in Action and during the subsequent years. That fostered a great love for, and full appreciation of, my need for God's Word in my life.

Dealing with "failure"

"Failure" to progress along that real or imagined line of healing is what has led many men and women to eventually give up the effort and return, often with a very heavy heart, to a life of homosexual behaviour. A number admitted to me that after ten or fifteen years of trying to change, they are simply worn out by the effort. And, while acknowledging that they don't believe that this is God's ideal for them, they have entered into a faithful, long-term relationship with a member of their own gender who also loves the Lord.

I neither condemn nor condone their actions; I simply understand. It is often too much to bear to not only feel you have failed in your life as a sinner, but to also feel as though you have failed in your efforts to change and conform to Christian "normality".

Does anyone travel the full length of this spectrum and reach the Holy Grail of heterosexual orientation that is sought by so many? There is no easy answer to this very important question. Over the years a number of Christian men and women have claimed a 100 per cent change in their desires and no longer experience any form of same-sex attraction. A larger number of people would profess to a significant change in SSA and have gone on to marry and enjoy a full and robust marriage. Some mention that they experience occasional periods of attraction towards their own gender, but openness with their spouse and a level of accountability with friends soon helps those times pass.

Other men and women I know experience the ebb and flow of attraction towards their own gender but, like other Christian singles committed to Christ, choose not to indulge in thoughts or act upon those temptations.

A turning point

There are certain moments in one's life that can be classified as defining moments: births, marriages, and the death of loved ones all fall into that category. In March 1999 I experienced one of those moments and it came as a revelation. In January of 1985 I had accepted the gift of salvation from our Lord Jesus Christ. I knew that part of my new life in Christ meant that I had to lay down my homosexual behaviour and live a life in keeping with the traditional biblical teaching that any form of sexual activity outside the boundaries of heterosexual marriage was sinful.

Based on that belief, and through several amazing God-incidences, I found myself, in January 1988, sitting in my first meeting at Love in Action, San Rafael, California, and hearing testimony that God can change the sexual identity and attractions of homosexually orientated men and women. By March 1999, some fourteen years after my conversion and cessation of homosexual activity, and some eleven years after first applying myself to orientation change, I had to accept the reality of my situation: for all of my desire and effort and application, I would still, if left to my own devices, be attracted to and fall in love with a woman.

This is not to deny that much of my life had changed for the good and that this change was not only in relation to God, but also in my relationships with both men and women. Over the years, and with great help, I had addressed many damaged areas in my life around the subject of gender and sexual identity issues. I was also fully aware of the many other areas that God was in the process of addressing that are common to all Christian men and women. But the one part that seemed untouched by God's presence in my life was the area of emotional and sexual attraction. No amount of biblical meditation or "taking every thought captive" or convincing myself what was meant by being a "new creation" in Christ accessed this dark recess. Piling Scripture, right behaviour, and good works on top of these real feelings and attractions did not mean that they went away. But it did mean that I had unknowingly isolated myself from this internal reality.

The decade had begun with the 1991 publication of *Out of Egypt: Leaving Lesbianism Behind*, citing my journey away from lesbianism, which prompted several years of a crazy ministry schedule around the world. From 1994, I began to experience depression and was admitted to the local psychiatric hospital early the next year; that was the first of three lengthy stays spread over the subsequent five years. I don't know what great thoughts you had as one millennium finished and another dawned. But in the year 2000, I had to face the truth that even though my behaviour was modified and I chose not to "think about how to gratify the desires of the sinful nature" as exhorted by the apostle Paul in Romans 13:14, my attractions and desires, if left unchecked, were still toward women and not toward men. I think Arthur Pink, an early twentieth-century English evangelist and scholar best describes my potential:

> Let all divine restraint be removed, and every man is capable of becoming, would become, a Cain, a Pharaoh, a Judas. How then is the sinner to move heavenwards? By an act of his own will? Not so. A power outside himself must grasp hold of him and lift him every inch of the way. The sinner is free, but free in one direction only – free to fall, free to sin. As the Word expresses it: "For when you were the servants of sin, you were free from righteousness" (Romans 6:20). The sinner is free to do as he pleases, always as he pleases (except as he is restrained by God), but his pleasure is to sin.[4]

Disappointment and freedom

The realization of this truth provoked two responses. The first was, unsurprisingly, one of disappointment as I had spent the best part of fourteen years trying to change my orientation.

The other response that manifested, however, took me quite by surprise. I felt unburdened by expectation and fully free to be myself! Did that new sense of freedom give me permission to go and find a gay Christian lady with whom I could live in

4   A. W. Pink, *The Sovereignty of God*, (Start Publishing LLC. Kindle Edition, 2012), p. 108.

a monogamous, faith-based relationship? Absolutely not! The freedom to be myself remained firmly within the constraints of traditional biblical teaching: that all sexual expression outside the realms of heterosexual marriage is sin. The freedom that I experienced back in the early part of the twenty-first century was to be released from the constraints of expectations placed upon me by myself, by well-meaning others, and by a Christian world-view that cannot cope with untidy and unresolved topics.

Statement of truth

The truth is that I haven't travelled from one end of the continuum to the other. I have not exchanged a homosexual identity for a heterosexual identity, and I haven't even *tried* to "change" for the past fourteen years. The relief has been exhilarating and has freed me to grow and mature as a concrete individual and not as an abstract identity.

I know that God cares about *me*.

I know that He cares passionately that I know I am loved and accepted by Him.

I know that He cares fervently that I love Him above all other things and that I extend our shared love toward other people.

I know that He cares that I live within His guidelines for my own good and for His glory.

Summer 2013

I can't recall the last Exodus International conference I attended, but I can be certain that there had been at least fifteen years between that and my arrival at Concordia University, Irvine, California, for, as it transpired, the last ever Exodus Freedom conference as it was now called. I hadn't followed this ministry's journey at all during those fifteen years and knew

21

nothing of the path that it had taken or was intending to take.[5] All I now knew was that the national umbrella ministry which had covered dozens of local ministries in its referral network no longer embraced the "reparative therapy" route or the goal of heterosexual marriage as the ultimate indicator of healing at the end of that path. Instead, it seemed to emphasize the way of discipleship as they walked alongside SSA men and women. This stance resonated with me, so I was pleased to accept the invitation to be one of their keynote speakers that year.

About two weeks before the meeting I was told that Exodus International (the old Exodus North America) would announce its impending closure at the conference. What word could I give to encourage those who may well be stunned, shocked, and perhaps even feel abandoned at this declaration? What hope could I offer these men and women, many of whom had travelled from Asia and Europe, that God is for them and with them as they journey along this path of holy obedience? Settling on Joshua 1:7 as my key text I began preparing a teaching around the theme "Be Strong and Courageous".

Summer 2014

One year on and I have just returned from speaking at a conference hosted by the Hope for Wholeness Network (HFW),[6] a ministry based in South Carolina, USA. Taking up the baton

5   It was only as I was researching for this chapter that I learned of the structural and name changes that had taken place during that time frame. The "old" Exodus International that I once knew had become Exodus Global Alliance and the 2013 conference that I attended was actually hosted by the once-named Exodus North America team.
6   The Hope for Wholeness Network brings together likeminded ministries, churches, counsellors, public speakers, and other organizations that stand boldly and graciously on the truth of Scripture with regard to homosexuality. This network also hosts a yearly conference that is open to all who are affected by or interested in this subject. More information on all the network offers can be found at www.hopeforwholeness.org.

that had been laid down by Exodus North America, the theme of the HFW conference was "Hope Rising". I was not privy to the thought process behind the choice of conference name, but I would not be surprised if part of the reason behind the title was to remind an individual that even though ministries and people may come and go, the promise of a new life in Christ Jesus remains eternal.

I reconnected with people from the previous year, renewed friendships from some fifteen years ago, plus met with men and women who were attending a conference such as this for the very first time. What I found so refreshing was that it didn't matter what subject was being addressed by the general session teacher, Jesus was lifted high and given His rightful place as the focus of our attention. As a result, many were given the gift of hope.

> May the God of hope fill you with all joy and peace as you trust in him, so that you may overflow with hope by the power of the Holy Spirit.
>
> **Romans 15:13**

Hope is an essential element that helps us to press forward and keep living in congruence with the moral mandates God has given us as Christians. But in recent years, many messages have detracted from a genuine hope in Christ for those of us with SSA, by bringing confusion or even injecting despair.

Mixed messages

There was a time when the Christian church largely spoke with one voice on the subject of homosexuality. Only sexual activity within the realm of heterosexual marriage (what other sort was there?) was acceptable, and all other single Christians, whatever

23

their orientation or attraction, were to remain celibate. How times have changed and now it is hard to find a consensus of opinion within a denomination, let alone contained in the body of Christ as a whole. On the subject of homosexuality it is, at times, hard to distinguish the Christian voice from that of the world as, in a desire not to offend, God's love is watered down into something so insipid it ends up being unpalatable to all.

In May 2014 the Reverend Mark Woods, a former editor of the *Baptist Times* in the UK, wrote an article reflecting on the difficulties the Baptist Union of Great Britain was experiencing as it tried to balance its traditional view on sexual expression while allowing each fellowship the freedom of self-determination. In an attempt to placate all sides of the debate, a statement was issued following the Baptist Assembly held in West Bromwich, England, thus prompting the article from Woods. He wrote:

> Of course, there are unresolved tensions in all this. Ministers are in principle allowed to conduct a same-sex marriage for someone else, but would be guilty of "conduct unbecoming" if they did it themselves. (The absurd situation might arise where a Baptist minister wanted to marry someone of the same gender in a service conducted by another Baptist minister; one would be disciplined, the other not. Seriously, it's bound to happen.)[7]

The Baptist denomination is not alone in offering mixed messages to its congregation. The United Methodist Church in America continues to dance around the subject and

7   Mark Woods, "How British Baptists have sort of allowed gay marriages but still aren't that keen on the idea", *Christian Today*, 20 May 2014 (http://www.christiantoday.com/article/how.british.baptists.have.sort.of.allowed.gay.marriages.but.still.arent.all.that.keen.on.the.idea/37560.htm).

displays amazingly nimble footwork as it side-steps certain denominational rules in order to placate the progressive element within Methodism. A recent statement from the traditional wing of the Methodist church[8] implies the dance is drawing to a close and a formal split in the United Methodist Church is inevitable.

The Church of England continues to duck and weave in an attempt to placate all points of view on the subject and succeeds only in intensifying the sense of frustration experienced by all irrespective of their position. The church's official line to the clergy is essentially, *you can share a home, a bank account, and even a bed, provided you do not express your love and commitment to one another in an act that is considered to be of a sexual nature.* It's like taking an alcoholic to a pub, giving him a pint of beer to hold, and making him promise not to take a sip for the duration of the visit. The rest of the clergy should try living according to those rules in their own heterosexual marriages. The Church of England is on a fruitless journey in seeking to combine the standards of this world with God's standard. And if they truly believed what they read, then they would know the futility of their endeavour. Jesus Himself prayed:

> My prayer is not that you take them out of the world but that you protect them from the evil one. They are not of the world, even as I am not of it. Sanctify them by the truth; your word is truth.

John 17:15–17

What has this increasingly liberal approach to sexual expression done for the gospel? Has it drawn myriads of sexually active single people flocking into church, hammering

8   "Regarding United Methodism's Future", *Good News*, 22 May 2014 (http://goodnewsmag.org/2014/05/regarding-united-methodisms-future/).

on the door, demanding a relationship with this all-loving God? What has this liberal approach done for discipleship? It seems that society's standards infiltrate and dictate church policy and determine the decision making of an average Christian far more than the Bible and 2,000 years of church history. As long as the church insists on fraying the edges of God's "bottom line", the lost will not be saved and the saved will not be encouraged to walk in the freedom that comes through faith.

The silent congregation

And yet, despite all the publicity and headlines advocating a reinterpretation of the Scripture, the majority of Christians who address issues of same-sex attraction *have not yielded* to the call to modernize (i.e., compromise) their thinking and embrace the life of a homosexually active Christian. Neither do they choose to live under the burden of having to have a heterosexual mindset in order to prove the power of Christ's life in them. This majority do not shout from the rooftops nor demand the right to be heard, and they are not vocally militant in their beliefs. These men and women go about serving in their local congregation, loving the Lord, and probably remaining silent about their personal issues for fear of being misunderstood if they admit to such struggles. Often the only voices they hear or articles they read advocate a joyful embracing of their gay identity within their faith, or a gut-wrenching condemnation of them along with the activity, or an enthusiastic call to change. All three positions can evoke a strong vocal response in their fellow parishioners, so is it any wonder the poor man or woman chooses to remain silent and live with their secret?

These silent men and women need to give voice to their lifestyle. As believers they have not chosen to become or to remain as gay-identified, but have fully embraced the task of bringing everything under the Lordship of Jesus and taken on the distinctiveness and freedom that comes from being Christ-identified. They may have experienced little to no change in same-sex attraction during the course of their Christian journey, but continue to remain faithful to biblical teaching despite the disappointment.

If you can recognize yourself in that last description then I want you to know that *you are not alone.* As I exhorted the men and women at that final Exodus conference in June 2013, I encourage you now, dear reader, to *take courage* as you learn to dwell in the land that you have been given. This is related to the Hebrew word *Chazaq* (pronounced "khä ˙zak"). This word can mean any of the following phrases:

- to strengthen
- to overcome
- to be strong and to become strong
- to be courageous
- to be firm and to grow firm
- to be resolute.

In Eugene Peterson's translation of the Bible, *The Message*, Joshua 1:1–19 captures the concept of *Chazaq*.

After the death of Moses the servant of God, God spoke to Joshua, Moses' assistant:

> Moses my servant is dead. Get going. Cross this Jordan River, you and all the people. Cross to the country I'm giving to the People of Israel. I'm giving you every square inch of the land you set your foot on – just as I promised Moses. From the wilderness and this Lebanon

east to the Great River, the Euphrates River – all the
Hittite country – and then west to the Great Sea. It's
all yours. All your life, no one will be able to hold out
against you. In the same way I was with Moses, I'll be
with you. I won't give up on you; I won't leave you.
Strength! Courage! [*Chazaq*!] You are going to lead
this people to inherit the land that I promised to give
their ancestors. Give it everything you have, heart
and soul. Make sure you carry out The Revelation that
Moses commanded you, every bit of it. Don't get off
track, either left or right, so as to make sure you get
to where you're going. And don't for a minute let this
Book of The Revelation be out of mind. Ponder and
meditate on it day and night, making sure you practice
everything written in it. Then you'll get where you're
going; then you'll succeed. Haven't I commanded you?
Strength! Courage! [*Chazaq*!] Don't be timid; don't get
discouraged. God, your God, is with you every step you
take.[9]

The Bible is full of encouragement for those who seek to follow
God, and Jesus Himself was one of the best cheerleaders
around! He encouraged people to step up to the challenge with
a word that is translated into Greek as *tharséō* – "be of good
courage, be of good cheer". This word is only used eight times
in the New Testament and on seven of those occasions it is used
by Jesus Himself:

I have told you these things, so that in Me you may have
[perfect] peace *and* confidence. In the world you have
tribulation *and* trials *and* distress *and* frustration; but be

9   Hebrew inclusion is mine.

of good cheer (*tharséō*) [take courage; be confident,
certain, undaunted]! For I have overcome the world.
[I have deprived it of power to harm you and have
conquered it for you.]

John 16:33, AMP[10]

This was not a word carelessly tossed around by the Lord, but
was reserved for those who really need the *rhema* word – the
"now" word – to press on. Jesus used *tharséō* to encourage the
woman who had suffered with a twelve-year bleed, for her faith-
filled persistence. He encouraged the paralytic to do something
he had never done before and walk, and He encouraged the
experienced sailors and fishermen to be confident in Him even
in the midst of a storm. Look again at what Jesus says about
overcoming this world and its difficulties in the Amplified Bible
paraphrase of John 16:33: "I have deprived it of power to harm
you and have conquered it for you."

Standing on the edge of something new

Forty years before God's statement in the first chapter of the
book of Joshua, we find Joshua, Caleb, and ten other men
were sent into Canaan to spy out the land that the Lord had
promised them. Although admitting that Canaan was fruitful
and even returning with concrete evidence of its fertility, ten
of the men were overwhelmed by the presenting difficulties.
They successfully convinced their fellow travellers that the
cost of taking the land was too high. For the next forty years,
that faithless generation of Hebrews wandered around the
wilderness until they had all died out, save Joshua and Caleb.
And it was them, along with a new generation of Hebrews,
who were to take up God's call.

10 Greek inclusion is mine.

Today I believe that the Christian church is standing on the edge of something new. In the last decade, ongoing discussions around civil partnerships, same-sex marriage, and gay adoptions have ensured that the subject of homosexuality has remained firmly in the public eye. During this time, the Christian voice has proved consistently inconsistent, resulting in confusion among the faithful. But I also believe that this is a time for Christian men and women who experience, to whatever degree, homosexual attraction to stand up and be pioneers within the faith. Daring to live openly as biblically obedient sons and daughters despite internal temptation and external pressure speaks to those within and without the church.

Present imperative

When Jesus used the term *tharséō*, He was commanding the disciples to remain *confident in Him and to their call,* even though they would experience trials and setbacks. Is Jesus commanding you, like the paralysed man, to do something you've never done before? Are you hearing the commandment not to fear, even though everything seems bent on dragging you down? Have you done everything you can to change your attractions and now, like the woman who touched the hem of His garment, do you hear Jesus command you to take Him at His word and move on?

Both the word *chazaq* that God speaks to Joshua and the word *tharséō* that Jesus uses are in the present imperative tense, meaning that they are exhorting someone to act *now*. Neither word can be mistaken for a suggestion or recommendation, nor is there scope for discussion but simply for obedience by Joshua and the New Testament characters. You are to be strong and courageous, the Bible writes, and you are to continue being strong and courageous.

Obedience

Obedience is one of the foundational pillars of discipleship and that requires us to face and deal with difficult and painful personal issues rather than withdrawing from them. In obeying God's commands, we need boldness to step out from the crowd, secular or Christian, and walk purposely in time to the beat of *His* drum. And in order to be bold and take courageous steps, we need confidence in the One who not only calls us but who walks with us and who sustains us along this journey of discipleship. As we begin journeying through this book, may I encourage you:

- *to not* conform to your old sinful patterns of thoughts and behaviours

- *to not* conform to world-views offered by a secular society or a theologically liberal church

- *to not* conform to expectations placed upon you:

  - by well-meaning friends who encourage you to step off the highway of holiness so that you can "be happy"

  - by well-meaning churches and denominations that just want you to hide away behind gender-affirming clothes, haircut, and behaviour (perhaps meant more for their own comfort than for yours)

  - by well-meaning Christian ministries and associations that want a neat and packaged believer who demonstrates healing and wholeness through certain behavioural guidelines.

Kingdom living

Pioneers are called to live lives entrenched in God's Kingdom. Kingdom living is scary and there are giants, both Christian and non-Christian, in the land! But Kingdom living is also fruitful.

> For the Lord your God is bringing you into a good land – a land with brooks, streams, and deep springs gushing out into the valleys and hills; a land with wheat and barley, vines and fig-trees, pomegranates, olive oil and honey; a land where bread will not be scarce and you will lack nothing; a land where the rocks are iron and you can dig copper out of the hills.
>
> **Deuteronomy 8:7–9**

Kingdom living is appealing. I find that I don't really care what other people think of me, as my focus is to please just one person, my heavenly Father. It is to Him alone I will have to answer the questions of what I have done with the gift of salvation and how I invested the talents He gave me. It will be He who determines whether I loved well or not. This book, *Dwelling*, is for those of us who choose to persist, even when the reality of our individual lives has not matched the hopes, the dreams, or the expectations that once spurred us on. We are privileged people, because in order for us to remain faithful followers of Christ we must continue to let the Holy Spirit search us, know us, dismantle, and repair us. Christ is our foundation, our cornerstone, and our capstone; it is in Christ alone we stand, dwell, and find rest. Whether your earthly life is or is not living up to the dreams and expectations you once held, it is good to know that this life *is not it.*

By an act of faith, Abraham said yes to God's call to travel to an unknown place that would become his home. When he left he had no idea where he was going. By an act of faith he lived in the country promised him, lived as a stranger camping in tents. Isaac and Jacob did the same, living under the same promise. Abraham did it by keeping his eye on an unseen city with real, eternal foundations – the City designed and built by God.

Hebrews 11:8–10, *The Message*

Chapter 2

Sexual Fluidity, Identity, and Generational Differences

> While the church should not change its teachings
> on matters of sexual morality, we have to change
> the assumption that correct teaching functions
> as pastoral care in its entirety. We can and must
> do more – and it begins by recognizing how our
> culture has created a sense of meaning, purpose,
> identity, and community that is tied to same-sex
> sexuality.[11]
>
> Mark A. Yarhouse, *Understanding Sexual Identity*

In December 2013 the young British Olympian diver Tom Daley used a five-minute posting on YouTube to reveal that he was in a relationship with a man and, as interesting as that was, I was more interested in what he didn't say rather than in what he did.[12] In his disclosure Daley does not identify himself as gay, nor does he claim that his orientation is gay, or that he is exclusively same-sex attracted. He states simply and, it has to be said, eloquently that right now, at this time in his life, he is in a physical and emotional relationship with a man. One could be cynical and suggest that his statement, "Of course I still fancy women", is a PR attempt to placate his many financial sponsors, or we could understand it to be a genuine reflection on the fluidity of sexual maturation.

11   Mark A. Yarhouse, *Understanding Sexual Identity: A Resource for Youth Ministry*, Grand Rapids, MI: Zondervan, 2013, Kindle edition.
12   See https://www.youtube.com/watch?v=OJwJnoB9EKw

At nineteen years old, the age Daley made this video, I was dating men while being overwhelmingly attracted to women. This was in the pre-internet days when you had to actually go to libraries and handle real books in order to find information on your topic of interest. In the mid-1970s, unfortunately, there was little in the reference section that could help me understand all that I was feeling, but there seemed to be a consensus of opinion that for many men and women, homosexuality was a passing phase in their ongoing sexual development. The writers of these hefty scientific tomes seemed to conclude that the majority of people moved on towards a full heterosexual future. Armed with such information, I waited for the journey to begin.

Unfortunately the expedition never really started and when I crossed the line from attraction into action and entered into my first physical relationship with a woman, my journeying took a completely new direction. In my estimation, my behaviour solidified not only my attractions but also my orientation and, eventually, my identity. By investing in the whole rather dubious triumvirate – attraction, orientation, identity – I firmly closed the door to the destabilizing questions and sense of uncertainty that had burdened me for so long. Accepting and embracing this bundle brought, for the first time in my nineteen years, a modicum of stability and a sense of belonging. In my opinion, I now knew who I was.

But times have changed and Tom Daley's five-minute video wonderfully encapsulates the sense that many of today's youth feel. He says towards the end, "I'm still Tom. I still want to win an Olympic gold medal in Rio 2016 for Great Britain." To the annoyance of many in the media, the Olympic diver does not label himself as anything other than the young and articulate man that he is, and we should take note.

Today's youth, whether that is in the realm of study, or career, or personal relationships would rather keep their options open than run the risk of being labelled and compartmentalized. And when it comes to the area of sexuality, some recent studies appear to be endorsing their rather open-ended stance.

Dr Lisa Diamond

When growing up, my attractions were almost exclusively toward the female, but when I was *confronted* with a pull towards a male, be that in real life or via the medium of television or film, I would consciously reject those feelings as being incongruent with my customary emotional response. In my ignorance I believed in the binary state of being either gay or straight and it never occurred to me that life could be tidal-like in its attractional ebb and flow. How different would my life have been if I had known then what is so widely understood today?

Dr Lisa Diamond is a professor of Psychology and Gender Studies at the University of Utah in the United States. A self-identified lesbian, Diamond describes herself as a "feminist scientist"[13] and, as a result of a longitudinal study on the fluidity of women's sexual behaviour, published her findings in 2009.[14] Her conclusions proved to be an eye-opener to all who read her book, irrespective of their social, religious, or political standpoint. An earlier study of hers, published in 2008,[15] highlighted quite sensational fluctuations in sexual orientation and identity among adolescents who originally identified as bisexual, all of which naturally challenged any claim that one's sexuality either in attraction, orientation, or identity is immutable. Diamond's study found that this fluctuation was much higher among the

13 http://www.feministvoices.com/lisa-diamond/
14 Lisa M. Diamond, *Sexual Fluidity: Understanding Women's Love and Desire*, Harvard University Press, 2009.
15 http://www.psych.utah.edu/people/files/diamond54a5.pdf

women rather than the men and it must be noted, somewhat surprisingly, that these vacillations and ultimately the long-term shifts towards heterosexual attraction and behaviour all occurred without consultation or therapy.

Diamond's latest work has been looking at male and adolescent sexuality in an attempt to confirm or disprove what she calls the three pillars of sexual fluidity:

- non-exclusivity (bisexuality)
- inconsistency between identity, attraction, and behaviour (i.e. self-identifying as heterosexual but admitting to some same-sex attraction and/or behaviour)
- variability over time (i.e. the gain or loss of SSA and the gain or loss of OSA – opposite sex attraction).

In a teaching given in October 2013 at Cornell University[16] Professor Diamond explains the findings she has to date and concludes that sexual fluidity is a general feature of human sexuality and is not specific to women. Diamond continues her summing up by stating that the sexual categories that are in common use, such as LGBTQI (Lesbian, Gay, Bi-Sexual, Transgender, Questioning [or sometimes used for Queer] Inter-sex) are useful mental shortcuts, "but we have to be careful in presuming that they represent natural phenomena".[17]

As an aside, a friend of mine recently attended a seminar where the acronym LGBTQQIAAPTS was used! That includes the following groups of people: Lesbian, Gay, Bi-Sexual, Transgender, Queer, Questioning, Inter-sex, Asexual, Ally, Pan-Sexual and Two-Spirit (an indigenous North American term to understand gender differentiation). Although that acronym

16   https://www.youtube.com/watch?feature=player_
embedded&v=m2rTHDOuUBw
17   Screen time: 38:55.

is impressive, it is nothing compared to the identity one can choose on one's Facebook profile in the US because, at the time of writing, one could select from fifty-eight possible gender identities. As one Facebook commenter said at the time of its launch back in February 2014, "Wow! That's more genders than Baskin-Robbins has ice cream flavors!"

Back to Professor Diamond. Finally, she concedes that her findings over the variability of attraction and behaviour can change quite significantly over time and that men (although fewer in percentage) and women can both experience significant long-term changes in their other-sex attractions. Diamond concludes: "…as a community, the queers have to stop saying: 'Please help us, we were born this way and we can't change' as an argument for legal standing."[18]

Dr Mark Yarhouse

Dr Mark A. Yarhouse is the Hughes Endowed Chair and Professor of Psychology at Regent University in Virginia Beach, Virginia, USA. There he founded the Institute for the Study of Sexual Identity (ISSI) in 2004 and continues today as its director. In recent years, Yarhouse's published research has been extremely helpful in helping men and women explore issues of sexuality from a Christian perspective. Part of his work has been directed toward the formation of identity and, I believe, dovetails nicely with Professor Diamond's work as briefly described earlier.

The particular body of work that I want to highlight and then illustrate is the "Three Tier Distinction", which the ISSI describes as follows:

18   Screen time: 43:15.

The Three Tier Distinction

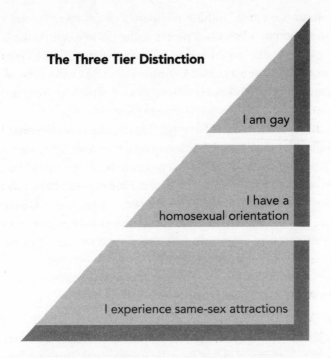

I am gay

I have a
homosexual orientation

I experience same-sex attractions

When we refer to the "three tier distinction," we are
talking about a distinction between same-sex attraction,
a homosexual orientation, and a gay identity. Same
sex attraction refers to experiences of physical and
emotional attraction to a person of the same sex. It
does not define a person. In fact, it is one of the most
descriptive ways to talk about a person's experiences.
Homosexual orientation describes the persistence
of attraction to the same sex. When a person speaks
of having a homosexual orientation, they are again
not necessarily defining themselves as a person, but
providing information about their same-sex sexuality
as an enduring pattern of attraction. When we think

about the word "gay" as an identity, we often refer to a person who adopts the word "gay" as who they are (rather than how they are). We recognize that there is a new generation of Christians who use gay more as an adjective to describe their sexual orientation, for example, a traditionally believing Christian who has a homosexual orientation might say, "I am a celibate gay Christian." Others, however, use gay to designate who they are (as identity) and others often assume through that identity label that the person views same-sex relationships as morally permissible.

The three tier distinction provides an alternative route to how one thinks about their identity and it can be useful to some people at certain points in their identity development. The [three tier] distinction would allow a person who experiences same sex attraction or a homosexual orientation to describe what they experience/feel without making a statement about their identity. Identity is a label that a person can choose for themselves, and different people have made different decisions about identity labels and their meaning. For example, some Christians have preferred to form their identity in Christ rather than referencing their same-sex sexuality. Others do both in referring to themselves as either a "gay Christian" or a "celibate gay Christian."

The three tier distinction should not be used to set an expectation that another person use descriptive language over an identity label. Rather, it is intended as a pastoral or counseling resource for those who find it helpful as they navigate sexual identity questions and concerns. [19]

19   Taken from http://www.sexualidentityinstitute.org/archives/13237

Putting meat on the bones

Using Yarhouse's model, I can then trace my own sexual and identity development.

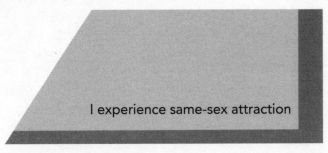

Having felt increasingly different from my own gender during my childhood years, around puberty I felt attracted to other girls and women. These attractions ranged from hero worship of particular teachers to increased sexual attraction toward fellow pupils.

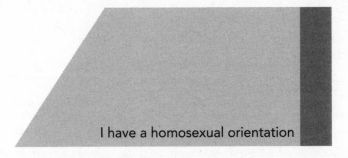

Realizing that these feelings were not diminishing with age but had become my default position, I dismissed any attraction towards the male gender as being an anomaly and slowly came to accept that my basic orientation was toward my own sex.

I am gay.

Once I entered into a same-sex relationship and began to invest in friendships with other similarly minded women, my orientation became the fulcrum around which my life revolved. My dentist was gay, I played for a gay hockey team and, eventually, about 90 per cent of all interactions outside of work were with gay-identified people. It was not a big step, therefore, to shift from a position of *what I do* (orientation) into *who I am* (identity).

Division and intervention

In my ignorance, I walked along this seemingly inevitable course towards an entrenched identity that was foundational to how I thought, who I interacted with, and my choice of life partner. But thanks to research over the past two decades, it seems that the good news for those youngsters currently experiencing attraction toward their same gender is that their future is not as fixed as once thought: they do have a choice.

Calling them "milestone events", Yarhouse divides up sexual identity development into five bands: awareness, behaviour, labelling, disclosure, and relationship. In his excellent book *Understanding Sexual Identity* and referencing earlier work done by Lisa Diamond and Savin-Williams,[20] Dr Yarhouse writes:

> In their review of studies of developmental milestones, Savin-Williams and Diamond noted that age of first awareness of attraction to the same sex occurs around age 9, while the age of first same-sex activity (usually defined as when one or both people in an encounter or relationship experience orgasm) occurs at an average age of between 14-17. The first experience of labeling as gay, lesbian, or bisexual occurs on average at age 16-18 years old. And disclosure to others typically occurs after that – at an average age of between 17-18. Most of the participants (86-95%) across the various studies reviewed of Gay young adults engaged in same-sex behavior – it was a normative aspect of their identity formation.[21]

What is important to make clear is that one cannot be rigidly formulaic in a child's development as there are so many variable factors that can help fashion an individual's maturation process. Interestingly, Yarhouse does make it clear that his studies with teenagers of faith have shown that they are less likely to adopt the identity of "gay" and the incidence of sexual behaviour is also lower than for those adolescents who claim no Christian faith.

As mentioned earlier, it is not my intention to dwell on the research and recent studies of same-sex attraction, as that is not

20   Ritch C. Savin-Williams and Lisa M. Diamond, "Sexual Identity Trajectories Among Sexual Minority Youths: Gender Comparisons" in *Archives of Sexual Behavior* 29, no. 6, 2000, pp. 607–27.
21   Yarhouse, *Understanding Sexual Identity*.

the remit of this book. However, I wholeheartedly encourage you to read Dr Yarhouse's publication as I believe it can help equip church congregations and pastors to better serve their children and youth. He offers thoughts and practical ideas on how one can offer alternative paths of thought and behaviour to those wrestling with their attractions and identities.

Male and female differences

In comparison to the wealth of study given to homosexual development in men, there has been a dearth of study focusing on the development of female same-sex attraction. I had very little published help back in the 1980s and much of the 1990s. Thankfully, times are changing and research is now finding significant differences between the two genders which, if the investigation continues, can only bring greater assistance to those women addressing sexual identification issues. I quote again from Yarhouse:

> There are some general differences we should point out between adolescent men and women here. For example, females tend to report that their attractions, sexual contacts, and adoption of a Gay-identity label are more of an emotional experience born out of an existing relationship with another female: [author quotes from another]. In contrast, adolescent males tended to more often report "explicitly sexual memories – feeling aroused by the sight of another boy in the locker room or experiencing a furtive sexual encounter with a male friend or cousin."[22] Another gender difference can be found in the

22 Author references Savin-Williams and Diamond, "Sexual Identity Trajectories Among Sexual Minority Youths: Gender Comparisons", p. 621 here.

timing of specific milestone events. In general, adolescent girls tend to adopt a Gay-identity label before engaging in same-sex sexual behavior, while adolescent boys tend to experience same-sex sexual behavior prior to adopting a Gay-identity label. Keep in mind, however, that these are more common trajectories rather than foregone conclusions. We found similar patterns in our more recent study of Christians. Males tended to report engaging in same-sex behavior at a younger age than when they labeled themselves as Gay. In contrast, females tended to be in a same-sex relationship at a younger age than when they reported engaging in same-sex behavior or labeling themselves as Gay. Again, it is important to stress that not all sexual minorities experience each of these milestone events. This appears to be particularly true when research focuses on Christian samples of sexual minorities.[23]

In the past mistakes have been made when people have taken majority findings to mean *all* of the people *all* of the time, resulting in poor counsel and direction. Therefore, I feel it right just to emphasize Yarhouse's caution: "Keep in mind, however, that these are more common trajectories rather than foregone conclusions."

Boomers, Gen Xers, and Millennials

In talking with Phil, whose testimony you will read later, I am mindful of the constant evolution of language that has taken place over the past fifty years. "In the 1960s and 70s, my teenage years," says Phil, "'gay' was only just beginning to

23   Yarhouse.

45

have a sexual meaning. Orientation still meant you were the right way up or upside down and the term same-sex attraction (SSA) just didn't exist. I first came across 'SSA' around 2002 and found, at last, a descriptive term that I could embrace, that accurately encapsulated all my feelings over the previous forty years."

Societal attitude toward same-sex relationships has almost changed beyond recognition and one has to remind oneself that in England and Wales, up until 1967, homosexual acts between consenting adults were still considered a criminal offence. Even in 2015, there are still a number of countries that consider homosexual behaviour worthy of imprisonment or even the death penalty. In the USA it wasn't until 1973 that homosexuality was declassified as a mental disorder, and other countries gradually followed their example over the subsequent years until it was finally declassified by the World Health Organization in 1990. China, however, waited until 2001 before removing it from their list of diseases, although same-sex desires remained listed as a source of mental distress for those unhappy with their orientation.

To be truthful, I'd never taken too much notice of the social groupings such as Gen Xers or Millennials until posting a question on the leaders' Facebook group page at the Hope for Wholeness Network. The essence of the question was that I had read one or two blogs from men and women who referred to themselves as "celibate gay Christians" and, as much as I tried, I could not understand why they insisted on identifying themselves as such. Why were they so keen to retain the label "gay"? The resulting discussion on the Facebook page revealed just how critical it is to listen for and understand a person's starting point if we are to engage productively in this important discussion on the trajectory of faith and sexuality.

A brief explanation

There are not specific years that define these generational structures and there are often two or three names by which each grouping is known. Interestingly, the upcoming generation of those born post-2000 are called Generation Z and are also known as the "Screenagers" or "Digital Natives" as they are the first generation to be born into and not to have had to adapt to the digital age. Although these groups are not an absolute science and are certainly open to discussion, the general breakdown that is relevant to this book is as follows:

Generation groups	**Years of birth**
The Baby Boomers	1943–1960
(subset: Generation Jones)	1954–1965
Generation X (*Baby Busters*)	1961–1978
	or 1964–1981
Generation Y (*Gen Y, Millennials*)	1982–1993
	or 1982–2004
Generation Z (*Screenagers, Digital Natives*)	1995–present
	or 2005–present

One online Forbes article I read said, "Most of what we hear about Gen Ys is negative. They have become synonymous with terms like tech-obsessed, entitled, impatient, and rule bending. While this certainly isn't the case for every Gen Y out there, many Gen Xers and Baby Boomers do find it difficult to work with them because their value systems appear to be so different."[24]

---

24 "Why I Love Gen Ys and You Should Too", 13 June 2013 (http://www.forbes.com/sites/work-in-progress/2013/06/13/why-i-love-gen-ys-and-you-should-to/).

Another article[25] impressed that while the Generation Xers (born between approximately 1961 and 1981) placed great importance on gaining a job for life, top British graduates today are "more likely to be attracted to working independently as a freelancer for multiple companies, than looking for a job for life with one employer". One study even showed "today's Generation Y (born 1982 to 1993) appear to be seriously questioning the nature of having a traditional job at all".[26]

Generation X, Y, and faith

All of the above may be dismissed as mildly interesting if it wasn't for the fact that these generational changes are not confined to the work place, but permeate every facet of an individual, including those of faith. The Pew Research Center is an impartial think tank based in Washington, D.C., USA. It provides information on social issues, public opinion, and demographic trends shaping the US and the world. As part of a broad study in 2014, it published the table below (the term "Silent" refers to the generation born before 1943):[27]

25 "Top Performing British Graduates Turned Off by Traditional Jobs", http://www.ibtimes.co.uk/top-performing-british-graduates-turned-off-by-traditional-jobs-1435195
26 "Top Performing British Graduates Turned Off by Traditional Jobs", http://www.ibtimes.co.uk/top-performing-british-graduates-turned-off-by-traditional-jobs-1435195
27 "How the Generations See Themselves", 5 March 2014, http://www.pewsocialtrends.org/2014/03/07/millennials-in-adulthood/sdt-next-america-03-07-2014-0-11/

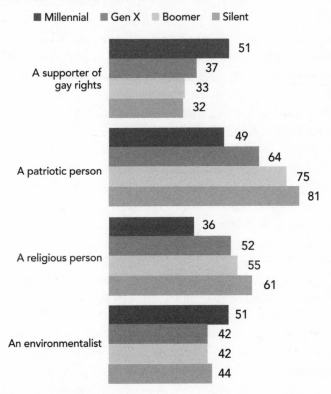

How the Generations See Themselves
% saying ... describes them very well

■ Millennial ■ Gen X ■ Boomer ■ Silent

A supporter of gay rights
- 51
- 37
- 33
- 32

A patriotic person
- 49
- 64
- 75
- 81

A religious person
- 36
- 52
- 55
- 61

An environmentalist
- 51
- 42
- 42
- 44

Note: Percentages reflect those who rated each description 8–10 on a scale of 1–10 where "10" is a perfect description and "1" is totally wrong.
Source: Pew Research survey, Feb 14-23, 2014
PEW RESEARCH CENTER

Based on the table above, it would be reasonable to presume the trajectory of results in each descriptive category will continue into the next generation and, perhaps, even beyond. This, I believe, will pose a challenge to those of us who hold not only that marriage is a sacred covenant between a man and a woman, but also that it is important to let go of any identity other than that of being "in Christ". I understand that we live in a post-modern age where relativism and individualism are applied to every aspect of life, and that truth and reality are often viewed simply in reference to our own personal history without any sense of universal application. Indeed, offering a sense of universal truth, God's Word for instance, as a foundation and template to life is largely dismissed as imperialistic rhetoric that promotes oppressive intolerance towards the marginalized in society.

I most certainly see the need to find connection with non-believers through listening to their language and terminology and by understanding their culture more fully. And I totally appreciate the importance of exploring the common ground we all share such as our need for security, identity, belonging, and purpose. Jesus did all of that when He walked the earth – but it was not for the purpose of joining them in their brokenness, but to call them out into their true identity and position in relation to Creator God, firstly through salvation and secondly through discipleship.

And this is why I find the confession of being a *celibate gay Christian* problematic. Rather than join a person in their sin identity, is it not our job to walk alongside, empathize, and assist the man or woman to discard the old grave clothes of sin – be that in attitude, identity, or behaviour – and live a life in keeping with the truth that we are a new creation in Christ (2 Corinthians 5:17)?

I asked my dear friend Nate, himself a Generation Xer, to briefly explain this change in people's thinking. He writes:

> You, Jeanette, and many of your generation with a
> similar background would use the word "gay" as
> something completely central to your selfhood; it was

50

something as fundamental to you as being white and female and needed to be discarded as you grew into a greater understanding of being a Christian. However, some believers who use LGBT labels do so not to define their identity, but to describe their experience. To use biblical categories, experiencing SSA (not lusting, but just experiencing SSA) is like suffering (C. S. Lewis actually referred to it as a disability), and some would say they aren't identifying with their "sin" when they use LGBT labels, but are just being honest about how deeply they experience the brokenness of creation within them.

Other believers would call themselves Gay Christians emphasizing the social component of identity. In other words, they want to stand in solidarity with those who do claim a gay identity and who have similar experiences to those that they have experienced. This would not only mean same-sex orientation, but also other social experiences such as feeling marginalized, disempowered, silenced, or shamed.

They would claim that we all stand united in our master identity (or "superordinate" identity, to use the language of social psychology) of being in Christ, but we are also identified by a myriad of other experiences/characteristics that categorize us into recognizable secondary social groups that are culturally meaningful in a particular context. Let me make it clear that they believe these secondary identities are certainly transformed by our superordinate in Christ identity, but that doesn't mean that they are nullified, or that their everyday significance is erased.

Where I stand

Words matter. It matters who I listen to and it matters what I tell myself. As I wrote in my introduction, there are, without doubt, many more conversations to be had and papers to be written on the subject of identity and faith. But, and I hope to explain why during the course of this book, I believe that there are a number of things that we believe about ourselves that are simply false and do much to harm our relationship with the Lord. Casting off our false beliefs and taking hold of who God says we are is critical to all believers, irrespective of their sinful disposition, if they are to mature in their faith.

God's command is to love Him with my whole heart, mind, soul, and strength. And in order to do that, I have to ensure that I am listening to and feeding off truth and not worldly opinion. If I rate society's assessment above God's Word, then I am not living out of the truth that I am a new creation, designed to become increasingly conformed to God's creational intent. The more I cling on to the vestiges of my old life – be that in thought, word, or deed – the more I hamstring my efforts to be transformed into the image of Christ. God's Word is clear:

> We demolish arguments and every pretension that sets itself up against the knowledge of God, and we take captive every thought to make it obedient to Christ.

> **2 Corinthians 10:5**

Unless God chooses to act miraculously, this change in attitude and outlook is not an overnight sensation, but a daily application of submission and response. Despite being imprisoned and facing innumerable trials and difficulties, the apostle Paul was able to pen the following:

Summing it all up, friends, I'd say you'll do best by filling your minds and meditating on things true, noble, reputable, authentic, compelling, gracious – the best, not the worst; the beautiful, not the ugly; things to praise, not things to curse.

Philippians 4:8, *The Message*

Chapter 3

Different Voices, Different Hymn Sheets

I n the last chapter we looked at some of the current research and noted that children and teenagers, from either gender, can experience great fluidity in their attraction and sexual identity development. We also noted the developing generational differences that not only exist in "the world" but are also prevalent within the church, thus requiring greater diligence in how we engage with each other when discussing sexuality. Before we look at specifics in our own lives, it would be pertinent to look at the current situation within Christendom.

A definitive position

I am told by various pastors that they are often asked questions by people who genuinely want to know the answers to the following:

- What is the biblical position concerning homosexuality?
- What stance does your denomination take?
- What position does your church take?
- What attitude does your congregation take?

Unfortunately, it is unlikely that the answers are going to line up in some neat row, as the church seems to offer nothing but mixed messages when it comes to homosexuality.

The confrontational church

There are the "confrontational"-type churches that seem rather keen to assign the subject of homosexuality as a "them versus us" situation. By adopting the language of the LGBT community a confrontational-type church actually falls into the trap of talking about "gays" as an ethnic group. Categorizing gay-identified people as a specific group is not supported by the Bible but does reinforce the gay community's desire to be recognized as a separate category and, therefore, the recipient of minority status.

Not only do confrontational churches play by the gay community's "rules", what I find more disturbing is that the most extreme of these churches seem to have forgotten that at the heart of this issue are real men and women. One often hears accusations of "those people" being engaged in promiscuity and reckless living, and considered unstable in all things.

I was once in a small group of Christian women whom I had known for about eighteen years, all of whom knew of my background. They had also attended a number of teachings I had given over the years. On one particular occasion, the tennis player Martina Navratilova had just announced her retirement from the professional circuit and had expressed a desire to have a child with her then partner. For some reason this came up in conversation and Alice (not her real name) bristled with indignation: "How can those kinds of people possibly want children?" Her tone was one of self-righteous disgust. And although I hadn't actually identified myself as being gay for many years, I felt a need to expose this ungodly response for what is was. "Alice," I said calmly, "I'm one of those kinds of people." Alice turned to me, smiled broadly and said jauntily, "No you're not, you're Jeanette," and resumed her discourse, oblivious to the impact her words may have had.

Hard-line attitudes and harsh words are often spoken by those who have failed to know, or choose not to know, the person or the name behind the identity. Other confrontational Christians and churches I have encountered imply that they want to see a tangible change in identity to prove a man or woman's Christian credentials. For some people, it seems that it's not enough for someone to stop homosexual activity but, for full integration into the "club", that person must prove that they no longer have those feelings. It's debatable whether they allow time for personal growth and the messiness and the possible failure that can often be part of the discipleship journey. Jesus said this about teachers of the law and Pharisees:

> They tie up heavy, cumbersome loads and put them on other people's shoulders, but they themselves are not willing to lift a finger to move them.
>
> Matthew 23:4

The compromised church

Some forty years ago, many Christian denominations, most churches, and the vast majority of believers would have upheld the traditional Christian position that sexual expression is to be within the context of heterosexual marriage. Faith-based ex-gay ministries sprung up around the world offering the hope that men and women struggling with various degrees of same-sex attraction could change through the power of Jesus Christ. Professional counsellors, many of whom were Christian, also offered therapy to individuals seeking help with their unwanted homosexual attraction.

All seemed very positive and hopeful but, over time, questions began to be asked within the Christian family. Individuals, many of whom had been in the vanguard of the ex-gay movement, began to question the "success rate" of this change process. Having watched men and women apply themselves and seemingly fail to change orientation or attraction, many leaders have taken a 180-degree about turn: some now actively embrace a greater pro-gay stance and are strongly encouraging Christians and churches to rethink their position.

There has been much change in society's stance towards homosexuality with the introduction of civil partnerships, followed soon afterwards by a change in the law allowing members of the same gender to marry.[28] The increased positivity towards homosexuality has put many denominations in quite a quandary. For instance, although the Methodist Church of Great Britain still upholds the sanctity of marriage as being between a man and a woman, the 2014 Conference agreed to engage in a two year conversation about whether the church should revisit the denomination's definition of marriage. In a list of *Frequently Asked Questions,*[29] the site declares clearly that an official blessing of a same-sex relationship would require formal liturgy and would not, therefore, be permitted on Methodist premises. However, in a bid towards inclusivity we read, "prayers of thanksgiving or celebration may be said, and there may be informal services

28   Although same-sex marriage has been legal in the Netherlands since 2001, a large number of countries worldwide have introduced Civil Partnership laws some years before making same-sex marriage legal. In the UK, the Civil Partnership Act became law in 2004 but it was a further ten years before a same-sex couple could be legally married. This act came into force on 13 March 2014. Federal law in the USA has, in the past, complicated matters pertaining to the legislation of same-sex partnerships. On 26 June 2015, however, there was a landmark ruling stating that all states must license and recognize same-sex marriages Not surprisingly, this law has not been welcomed unequivocally by every US citizen in all fifty states.
29   http://www.methodist.org.uk/who-we-are/views-of-the-church/human-sexuality/talking-of-marriage-and-relationships/same-sex-marriage-frequently-asked-questions

of thanksgiving or celebration."[30] Compromised Christianity is seemingly indistinguishable from today's pleasantly liberal and well-meaning middle class.

The Methodists are not alone. There are a number of other denominations around the globe locked in discussion regarding their current stance on homosexual behaviour and legally accepted same-sex relationships. One large point of discussion is the question of how one welcomes the individual without affirming their behaviour. It is in this area that we see the greatest contamination of the biblical understanding of love. The message from Christians who consider homosexual behaviour in a positive light is that saying no to some behaviour is indicative of not loving someone. And because God is love and loves all people He would not restrict a behaviour that brought so many people real happiness. Yet anyone who has looked after small children knows that that belief system is clearly not true. Because we love the child we will do everything in our power to keep them safe and that includes saying "no" to certain behaviours.

Similarly, if the church believes that an individual flourishes best when he or she follows the maker's handbook, the Bible, the church must believe that it is not unloving but life-enriching to speak against any behaviour that contravenes God's intent. The world-view has knitted together love, acceptance, and affirmation and presented it as a single unit. Unfortunately, the compromised church is following suit and, in so doing, short-changing the man or woman who is in search of Truth.

30 Ibid.

The confused church

I think the largest number of Christians and church leaders probably fall into the "confused church" category. There have been so many changes in societal attitudes to homosexuality over the past fifty years that many no longer know what to believe. Even if the church adheres to God's creational intent laid out in Genesis 2, the leaders may well have a congregation who do not hold to a similar stance. A good number of today's believers were not brought up in a church environment and are really only cognisant of society's understanding of sexuality.

There will also be a proportion of Christians who are experiencing some level of SSA or may have one or more family members who are openly gay. And even if they don't know of someone in their family, then it is still highly likely they have good friends or work colleagues who are quite open about their sexuality.

On a human level, and in this general atmosphere of individualism, one can understand the congregation's often asked question, "Who are we to deny people love and companionship?" So, in the confused church, the problem is that compassion starts to override biblical morals, and history seems to show that the endpoint of that pathway is almost always the compromised church. In my experience I have found that a lack of Bible-based preaching and a congregation that are not encouraged to read God's Word for themselves is the real problem at the core of a confused church.

Can I be a "gay Christian"?

This question results in a multitude of answers, depending on who you are asking and what level of identity and activity you are referring to. I do not have any qualifications as a Bible scholar, a counsellor, or a scientist. I come simply as a punter in the pew who has spent the past thirty years trying to live positively in accordance with the teachings found in the Bible and in that spirit I offer my opinion.

> If you declare with your mouth, "Jesus is Lord," and believe in your heart that God raised him from the dead, you will be saved. For it is with your heart that you believe and are justified, and it is with your mouth that you profess your faith and are saved.
>
> **Romans 10:9–10**

My point of conversion was delayed for several months because God, through His Holy Spirit, had made it clear to me that engaging in active homosexuality was not compatible with living a life committed to Jesus and in obedience to biblical teaching. This was not what I wanted to hear. At the time, I was fully immersed in a relationship with a wonderful woman with whom I truly wanted to spend the rest of my life; she was everything I had ever hoped for and more. She also happened to be a born-again Christian, and it was through her that I had begun to go to church and explore the Christian faith.

In the end, however, I felt I had to make a decision. God was either who He said He was in the Bible and, therefore, demanded obedience, or He was *not* God, thus allowing me to turn away from all biblical teaching and walk down a path of my own choosing. Once convinced that God is the great "I Am", I knew that to ignore His offer of salvation through faith in Jesus would result in everlasting separation from all good things. Faced with such a prospect, then, my conversion was a *fait accompli*.

It was with a very heavy heart and with many tears of sorrow that I committed my life to Christ, knowing that this decision meant turning my back not only on someone I loved and the only way of life that I had ever known, but also on all that seemed completely natural to me. There were many things that God did *not* point out about my life prior to my conversion that were just as sinful, in His sight, as my homosexual behaviour. But I confessed the sin that was made known to me *at the time*. Over the subsequent thirty years, the Holy Spirit has faithfully pursued His habit of pointing out everything else that hinders my relationship with God!

But this is not the story of all men and women who are engaged in homosexual relationships and come to Christ. Just like many heterosexually active men and women who are given the faith for salvation, some sexually active lesbians and gay men are not convicted of this particular sin prior to becoming a Christian. And that is OK. Over the years, I have seen the Holy Spirit working His purpose out in men and women from all kinds of backgrounds in His own good time. As the apostle Paul writes: "continue to work out your salvation with fear and trembling, for it is God who works in you to will and to act in order to fulfil his good purpose" (Philippians 2:12–13).

Unfortunately, I find that too many Christians speak as though God has abdicated and appointed them in His place to determine who is saved and who is lost and bound for hell. This is especially so in the area of broken sexuality. I suggest we let God get on with His job as we walk alongside, encouraging the believer in the ways of the Lord and giving the Holy Spirit space to do the convicting of sin. Is this a messy course of action? Absolutely, but I have found that behaviour modification to please others is only a temporary state built on a foundation of sand. It is quickly destroyed when the storms and challenges of life strike a given individual. Conviction by the Holy Spirit and repentance by the believer, irrespective of their feelings, places the person on the same side as God and creates a firm foundation on which the man or woman can stand the buffeting of the various storms. In his book *Love Beyond Reason*,[31] John Ortberg writes:

> It is in the storm that the soundness of the house is revealed. A foundation is not a glamorous thing. No one visits a house and says, "What a great foundation you have here." No one even knows. Until the storm.

At those times when feelings of loneliness have nearly overwhelmed me and a future without the intimate companionship of another has placed me on the brink of despair, I have been able to go back to the point when I stood in agreement with God and *stand* until the storm eventually subsides and a certain peace returns. Every person deserves the chance to *stand firm* under the onslaught of the world and their desires. We do a disservice to those SSA men and women by insisting on their behaviour modification, such as modifying acts of endearment toward their partner, without waiting for the conviction of sin, just so we can keep our Christianity in a neat and tidy package. It may make the congregation feel comfortable around them if they keep their SSA non-obvious and unmentioned so that they "pass as straight", but what does such suppression and conformity to other people's programmes do to the spiritual life of SSA men and women?

31   John Ortberg, *Love Beyond Reason: Moving God's Love from Your Head to Your Heart*, Grand Rapids, MI: Zondervan, 1998. Kindle edition, p. 85.

What about the "gay Christians" who condone homosexual activity?

Identity, orientation, and activity are not one and the same thing, although some people try to make the case that they are; this is where much confusion comes in. My understanding is that someone being "gay-identified as a Christian" is not the same thing as being a "Christian with SSA". And even within both those categories – the former emphasizing identity and (often) community, the latter emphasizing orientation and temptation – you will find some who actively engage in homosexual behaviours and others who do not. Some see sexual activity as the fulfilment of their identity whereas others see sexual activity as falling prey to their temptations. Then there are some with SSA who have neither embraced a gay identity nor acted out their proclivities. So, it is crucial to listen carefully to what people say when they speak of "gay Christians", and discern what it is *they* mean by the term.

There are a number of gay-identified men and women who are aware of the Scriptures and generally accepted Christian teaching on homosexuality, but believe that their homosexual behaviour is completely compatible with their Christian faith. They bring another interpretation to biblical texts and pursue the course of a monogamous faithful relationship with a fellow believer of the same sex.

While I disagree wholeheartedly with that stance and find their biblical exegesis shaky, I will not be addressing the reasoning behind their beliefs. There are, however, a number of helpful resources on the market and I certainly recommend Joe Dallas's book *The Gay Gospel?*[32]

32   Joe Dallas, *The Gay Gospel? How Pro-Gay Advocates Misread the Bible*, Eugene, OR: Harvest House, 2007. This is an updated version of his 1996 book, *A Strong Delusion*.

What about the "gay Christians" who remain celibate?

There are a number of Christians like Wesley Hill who are finding a voice within the Christian community. Wesley Hill describes himself as a gay-identified Christian who upholds the traditional biblical teaching that sexual expression is only permitted between a man and a woman within the context of marriage. Therefore, Hill argues, a gay-identified Christian is to practise celibacy and he encourages the believer to seek a life of intentional community in which he or she can experience some respite from the loneliness and sense of exclusion that they may otherwise feel. Hill is the assistant professor of Biblical Studies at Trinity School for Ministry in Ambridge, Pennsylvania, USA, and is also a frequent contributor to the blog site Spiritual Friendship.[33] He is also the author of *Washed and Waiting*.[34]

Hill pulls no punches in describing the cost of commitment experienced by those men and women choosing this path, and for inspiration and illustration, he draws heavily on the writings of Henri Nouwen and Gerard Manley Hopkins, both Catholic and homosexual-identified celibates. Towards the end of the book Hill writes:

> The Bible calls the Christian struggle against sin faith (Hebrews 12:3–4; 10:37–39). It calls the Christian fight against impure cravings holiness (Romans 6:12–13, 22). So I am trying to appropriate these biblical descriptions for myself. I am learning to look at my daily wrestling with disordered desires and call it trust. I am learning

33   See http://spiritualfriendship.org/
34   Wesley Hill, *Washed and Waiting: Reflections on Christian Faithfulness and Homosexuality*, Grand Rapids, MI: Zondervan, 2010, Kindle edition.

to look at my battle to keep from giving in to my temptations and call it sanctification. I am learning to see that my flawed, imperfect, yet never-giving-up faithfulness is precisely the spiritual fruit that God will praise me for on the last day, to the ultimate honor of Jesus Christ.

My continuing struggle for holiness as a gay Christian can be a fragrant aroma to the Father. I am coming to believe that it will be, in C. S. Lewis's words, "an ingredient in the divine happiness."[35]

I have to confess that, as insightful as the book was at times, I found *Washed and Waiting* rather depressing. I doubt the author would agree with me, but *the impression I was left with* was that in identifying as a "gay Christian", Wesley Hill had locked himself into a cul-de-sac existence rather than embarking on a journey towards something greater and more enriching. There seemed to me a sense of treading water while waiting for heaven, instead of embracing the believer's position of being seated in the heavenlies *now* and enjoying and exploring the ramifications of that truth through our life here on earth.

We will look at the subject of "gay-identified" in more depth later on. But for now, let's look at the larger concept of identity and what we use to integrate how we perceive the core of who we are: is it our sins (behaviours), our problem (orientation), or our Saviour (Christ as advocate, healer, and goal of our transformation)?

35   Ibid., p. 146.

Sin-identified, problem-identified, or Christ-identified?

My earliest thoughts about identity were those of an awareness of feeling different from my siblings and schoolmates. The older I became, however, my feelings gradually morphed from being *different from* into feeling *attracted to* members of my own gender and further evolved into a desire to live in a full relationship with another female. I entered into my first gay physical relationship at the age of nineteen and life finally made sense. I felt as though I had come home and fully embraced my identity as being gay.

In truth I have self-labelled for most of my life, labouring for many years under the belief that I was "uncared for" and "unloved". From the age of sixteen, I also took on the label of "gay" for about ten years. I followed that by another ten years self-labelled as "ex-gay". The label "ex-gay", however, seemed to become more uncomfortable as the years progressed and, although I wasn't engaging in any sexual behaviour, I could never really shake off the feeling that if God were to one day change His mind and decide that homosexual behaviour was now OK by Him, I would not ask for a second opinion!

On reflection, I can see how little I understood about the concept of being a new creation in Christ (2 Corinthians 5:17) in theory, let alone embracing it as truth and in practice. I don't say that in a self-condemnatory way, but in appreciation of how God's Holy Spirit guided me, very patiently, into this truth. For not only had I to come to terms with my sexual identity, but I also had to confront my gender identity in light of my new-found faith. For the first four years of my Christianity I would only ever accept and describe myself as a Christian *person*, refusing categorically, and to the confusion of other believers, to consider myself as a Christian *woman*.

Moving on from being sin-identified as "gay" into being problem-identified as "ex-gay" proved helpful at first. It reminded me that I was under new ownership and obligated to pursue God's way as laid out in the Scriptures. However, over time, the "ex-gay" tag became more burdensome. It didn't really reflect my true state, and I'm sure it was a factor in an episode of severe depression that lasted for a number of years.

Towards the end of that time, I decided to stop trying to change my orientation to fix my problem. And so I threw away my "ex-gay" label and became just me – a Christian woman. No more and no less. For the next fifteen years, despite intermittent ebbs and flows of emotional dependency (that is, enmeshment in the emotional aspects of friendships with other women), I just got on with life. However, since the Exodus Freedom Conference in the summer of 2013, God has been leading me back into ministry in this particular area of broken sexuality, and especially regarding identity.

What are you? Where do you stand? People seem intent on attributing labels in order to clarify the different standpoints on this issue of sexuality and the Christian. As reticent as I am to stick another label across my forehead, I can understand people's need for clarification in this extremely emotive and sometimes hostile environment. That is why I was intrigued when I came across the phrase "post-gay".

Canterbury Tale

The Reverend Peter Ould is a Church of England priest, a consultant statistician, and a one-time blogger with an interest in the topic of human sexuality. You can read the archive of his writing at www.peter-ould.net. In his 2007 online article, "You and Me Together",[36] Ould outlines some

36   Peter Ould, "You and Me Together", 19 April 2007 (http://www.peter-ould.net/2007/04/19/you-and-me-together/).

of the problems with the term "ex-gay", referring to it as a bi-polar model that implies an individual has completely passed from one state – gay – into another state – ex-gay. While admitting that for some men and women it may well be the case that they no longer harbour any same-sex attraction, the majority of people do not conform to this either/or model and are located somewhere in the space in between. In order to engage this middling majority, Peter Ould coined the phrase "post-gay".

> Post-gay isn't an ontological statement, it's a vectorial statement. For those uninitiated in the deeper arcane magicks of mathematics, a vector is simply a description of a direction and magnitude. It describes a movement, not a position (which is ontology). Post-gay then is less about being straight or gay and rather about a choice of a journey.[37]

He goes on about this trajectory to write:

> This is why post-gay is a far better description for those who have left homosexuality behind. It describes a journey away from a false identity constructed around one's emotions and a true one constructed in following Jesus. For some of us that journey involves changes in our sexual orientation, perhaps marriage and kids. For others they see no change in their sexual attractions, but they have left behind the place of false-identity, of seeing themselves as "gay" and that as a defining unchangeable aspect of their being.[38]

37   Ibid.
38   Ibid.

Pro-active journeying as a "post-gay Christian"

As loathe as I am to take hold of yet another label, Peter Ould's phrase seems more like a ticket to somewhere rather than merely being a location marker. It resonates with the whole Christian ethos of pilgrimage and the transformation of every sojourner from one state of glory into the next (2 Corinthians 3:18). It gives hope to the man or woman who chooses to be a faithful follower of Christ and has left the starting point of gay, but has "failed" to cross the finishing line of ex-gay and has been left, often for years, floundering somewhere in the middle with neither stance clearly in sight.

While using the phrase as an adjective rather than a noun, the post-gay Christian can walk transparently and authentically towards the goal of being fully Christ-identified. This approach is, I believe, a win-win position for individuals with SSA, and for the people and churches seeking to understand and walk alongside them. For surely this journey with Jesus toward Christ-likeness is not just for the few addressing same-sex attraction issues, but is the walk to be undertaken by all believers, irrespective of their particular story? This sense of journeying towards the common goal of Christ-identification helps combat the often-held belief that those addressing same-sex issues are somehow vastly different from any other Christians addressing residual sin in their lives.

Being able to vocalize the issues faced in this "post-gay" journeying grants greater freedom for the individual. And what is freedom? For me, freedom is not the lack of desire for something or someone; it is the absence of compulsion. Freedom is the introduction of choice.

> But if we live in the light, as God is in the light, we can
> share fellowship with each other. Then the blood of
> Jesus, God's Son, cleanses us from every sin.
>
> 1 John 1:7, NCV

Confused?

There may have been a time when Christ's body, the church, spoke with one voice regarding homosexuality and Christianity, but it is clear that this is no longer the case. At the time of writing there appear to be four major options available to the Christian with same-sex attraction.

- The first group encourage you to embrace your SSA as a fundamental part of your identity and, using their own interpretation of Scripture, condone homosexual behaviour within the context of a life-long monogamous union. (This approach integrates identity, orientation, and activity around being gay. Problems often arise when Jesus becomes simply an add-on or is parallel to the gay identity, and not the only person of our worship.)

- The second group embrace "gay" as their identity (a gay Christian), but do not condone homosexual activity as a biblical expression of God's created intent. A gay Christian would, therefore, choose to live as a celibate. (This approach integrates identity and orientation, but not activity. The problem here is that it fuses identity and orientation in a way that makes it seem as if they should be part of the "gay community" but they aren't. The fusion is confusing.)

- The third group would be more likely to refer to themselves as "ex-gay". They do not see homosexuality as something to embrace either as an identity or a behaviour. Believing

70

fully in God's created intent of sexual intimacy only within heterosexual marriage, the third group encourage a person to pursue a path that may well include various therapeutic methods working towards a significant change in orientation. (This approach centres around SSA orientation, but not with gay identity or activity. Problems can arise if heterosexuality and [often] marriage becomes the goal instead of Jesus. This means that there is danger of a person succumbing to behaviour modification that makes it look as if they've achieved their goal, instead of submitting to the Word and the Spirit in order to encounter internal transformation to Christ-likeness.)

- The fourth group are not too far from the third group, inasmuch as they also consider that a believer is not to embrace "gay" as their identity or to engage in homosexual behaviour. While adhering to God's created intent, the fourth group do not see heterosexuality as a goal in life, but rather Christ-likeness. So they would see any change in orientation and attraction as a welcome side effect of their pursuit in becoming more fully Christ-identified. (This approach centres around Christ, and not gay identity, orientation, or activity – or the false goal of heterosexuality. No problem here, at least not on the SSA issues.)

The strength of being "post-gay"

Based on the list above, I would consider the fourth group to come under the title "post-gay". If one must be labelled for clarification, then I believe post-gay gives the freedom of experiencing SSA, however frequent or infrequent, mild or severe, without feeling as though that is the sum total of one's existence. It is something I experience – *but it is not, and never will be, who I am*. This term throws off the shackles of being sin-identified

71

or problem-identified. It offers every believer the chance to walk in the *newness* of life that comes from being born again into this outrageous identity of heir and co-heir with Christ.

> Jesus, once more deeply moved, came to the tomb. It was a cave with a stone laid across the entrance. "Take away the stone," he said. "But, Lord," said Martha, the sister of the dead man, "by this time there is a bad odour, for he has been there four days." Then Jesus said, "Did I not tell you that if you believe, you will see the glory of God?" So they took away the stone. Then Jesus looked up and said, "Father, I thank you that you have heard me. I knew that you always hear me, but I said this for the benefit of the people standing here, that they may believe that you sent me." When he had said this, Jesus called in a loud voice, "Lazarus, come out!" The dead man came out, his hands and feet wrapped with strips of linen, and a cloth round his face. Jesus said to them, "Take off the grave clothes and *let him go.*"
>
> **John 11:37–44, emphasis mine**

Like Lazarus, we may have walked out of the tomb still clothed in the vestiges of death, but it is not God's intention that we remain in them as some misplaced badge of honour. On that first Easter Sunday, Peter and John entered Jesus' tomb and found *all* the burial cloths that had been wrapped around Christ's body. Jesus had left *all* traces of death behind Him as He rose from the grave that morning and that, surely, is our call? We can choose to identify with Lazarus and respond to Jesus but still carry the fabric of sin and death around with us, or we can identify with Christ and embrace the fullness of life that is on offer. Paul refers to this opportunity as follows:

> We were therefore buried with him through baptism into death in order that, just as Christ was raised from the dead through the glory of the Father, we too may live a new life.
>
> **Romans 6:4**

Paul later writes:

> And God raised us up with Christ and seated us with him in the heavenly realms in Christ Jesus, in order that in the coming ages he might show the incomparable riches of his grace, expressed in his kindness to us in Christ Jesus.
>
> **Ephesians 2:6–7**

A transformed life attracts attention

> Meanwhile a large crowd of Jews found out that Jesus was there [at Simon the Leper's house] and came, not only because of him but also to see Lazarus, whom he had raised from the dead. So the chief priests made plans to kill Lazarus as well, for on account of him many of the Jews were going over to Jesus and believing in him.
>
> **John 12:9–11**

A transformed life attracts attention. Some people are curious just for the sake of it, some want to know more about this chance to be transformed, and some want to destroy all that a life with Christ entails. In being raised from the dead and then engaging publicly with Jesus Lazarus opened himself up to a raft of responses and potential danger as, indeed, did his Master.

Isn't this what the church should expect? Aren't we all "post something", walking towards the fullness of life in Christ?

73

Since it is so, shouldn't all church members be walking shoulder to shoulder, *us and us* – not *us and them* – transparent and transforming in one common pursuit of bringing glory to God? All of us, whatever our weakness, may still encounter pockets of resistance from the world and our own flesh. But if we can treat wayward thoughts, feelings, and temptations according to what they are, the side-effect of living in a sinful world, we will be less inclined to embrace them as the sum total of our life. It is Truth that sets us free to walk in freedom.

> Since, then, you have been raised with Christ, set your hearts on things above, where Christ is, seated at the right hand of God.
>
> **Colossians 3:1**

Dwelling in the Land is, essentially, a book about discipleship. In the next chapter we will look at the necessity of living in accordance with God's two greatest commandments for those who follow Jesus Christ.

Section 2

What do we actually believe? How does our thinking influence our Christian walk? Are our expectations in keeping with biblical teaching, or have we allowed worldly reasoning too much influence?

Chapter 4
Prisoners of Hope

> *When God chooses, he also redeems; when God chooses and redeems, he also works in people's lives; and the miracle of the divine–human relationship, from the very beginning, has always been that human thought, will and action is somehow enhanced, rather than being cancelled out, by the divine initiative and power.*[39]
>
> Tom Wright, *Revelation for Everyone*

Testimonies of change

How many testimonies of changed lives have you read over the years? How many small groups and big conferences have you attended that have given you a deeper understanding of our awesome God? And how much of that understanding has spurred you on to pray for a significant change in the area of same-sex attraction?

What has been the long-term result of these prayers? Has your hope of change remained constant throughout this process, or has it swung from dizzying heights to unfathomable depths, depending on the magnitude of attraction and temptation you encounter, and your success, or otherwise, in resisting the enticement?

Over the past few years a number of books and television documentaries have featured men and women who have tried to change their orientation from gay to straight and, in their estimation, have not only failed to achieve success

39 Tom Wright, *Revelation for Everyone (New Testament for Everyone)*, London: SPCK Publishing, 2011, Kindle edition, p. 185.

but have also been harmed in the process. Their response to this failure is as varied as the individuals who attempted the transformation in the first place. But an organization, Beyond Ex-Gay,[40] conducted a survey that began in September 2011 and concluded at the end of November 2012. Their aim was to gather the thoughts of men and women who had experienced some measure of therapy, professional or otherwise, in an effort to address their same-sex attraction. Although 417 participants from a variety of backgrounds and ethnicity completed the survey, the bulk of the participants classified themselves as white gay males.[41]

Three questions

Beyond Ex-Gay's survey comprised a number of questions offering multi-choice answers. It also gave opportunity for the participants to add their personal comments at the end of each section. The men and women were able to check as many answers to each question as they felt were applicable. In the box below, I have selected the three questions (numbers 6, 7, and 8 respectively) that I felt were most relevant to my book and give the top three answers:

What were the reasons (the motivations) you tried to follow an ex-gay path?[42]

1. To be a better Christian

2. I believe it's what God wanted me to do

3. I feared I would be condemned by God

40 "Beyond Ex-Gay is an online community and resource for those of us who have survived ex-gay experiences" – see http://www.beyondexgay.com/.
41 See http://www.beyondexgay.com/survey/results/demo.html#Q14.
42 Survey taken from http://www.beyondexgay.com/survey/results.html.

What were you hoping to get from (the results you wanted from) your ex-gay experience?

1. To be straight
2. That the nagging SSA would go away
3. To be closer to God

What significant experience motivated you to quit the ex-gay movement?

1. It didn't make me straight
2. I was exhausted
3. I realized God loved me regardless of my sexuality

The top answer to this third question was nearly off the scale (302) and the other answers were low in comparison (202 and 201 respectively).

Prisoners of expectation

The results of these three questions came as no surprise to me. As mentioned earlier in the book, I too had become exhausted by the fifteen-year process of trying to change my orientation. It was only when I laid that down and accepted the truth that change seemed to be, for me at least, an elusive goal that I began to sense a palpable difference in my life. I hadn't realized how weighed down I had felt by this expectation to change and that this burden had affected and infected so much of my day-to-day living. An unexpected outcome of being my real self in Christ rather than an "aspirational self" was a significant reduction in attraction or temptation or anything that could have been placed under the heading "homosexual"! It would be fair to say that I had been set free from being a fifteen-year "prisoner of expectation" and became a lifelong "prisoner of hope".

The term "prisoner of hope" is not something I created, but is a phrase that jumped out at me some six months ago when I was reading the book of Zechariah:

> As for you, because of the blood of my covenant with you,
> I will free your prisoners from the waterless pit.
> Return to your fortress, you prisoners of hope;
> even now I announce that I will restore twice as much
> to you.
>
> Zechariah 9:11–12

Comments from the waterless pit

As I read through the comments and testimonies that accompanied this survey, it was clear that, whatever their primary motivation, most of these Christian men and women had tried very hard to change their natural inclination toward SSA into a disposition that better reflected that of traditional Christianity. One couldn't help but feel compassion when reading personal journeys that were birthed in hope – an expectation even – of change, but then transition towards disillusionment and sometimes even despair. What was most distressing was to read how their disenchantment with either the speed of change or the seeming complete lack of change significantly impacted their understanding of God, His ways, and His church. There were stories of some people leaving the Christian faith altogether, while others stepped away from established Christianity and its people, claiming that the combination instilled in them only a profound sense of shame. What did become clear was the large number of men and women who have changed their theology in order to fit the way they feel. If I could sum up their thoughts and combine them with other comments I have encountered over the years the collective statement would read something like: "If, even after all this effort, I haven't changed regarding SSA then there is nothing to change. God is happy as I am. Therefore, I will embrace my homosexuality and worship God within a faithful, monogamous same-sex relationship."

I have been connected, in varying degrees, with the Ex-Gay Movement for the past twenty-seven years and have shared offices, platforms, and my life with a number of men and women who now live according to the statement above.

What has gone wrong?

What has gone so wrong that not only individuals but also ministries and denominations have shifted their position on this subject of homosexuality? Could it be that these dear brothers and sisters have unwittingly shifted their hope from the personhood of Jesus to that of a personal outcome: a change in orientation, attraction, and behaviour? In seeking to bring a "besetting sin" under the Lordship of Christ, is it possible that they have lost sight of the bigger eternal picture and ended up with a skewed understanding of their relationship with God and their position in Christ?

Although many would claim that they now live in an enlightened state, have these believing men and women imperceptibly travelled from being a *prisoner of hope* to becoming a *prisoner of doubt*, a *prisoner of despair* or even, through the deception of the evil one, a *prisoner of false hope*? How do you and I protect ourselves and each other from falling into the same trap, and how do we help those who are now what I believe to be *prisoners of false hope* and realign them with the truth?

Zechariah in context

Zechariah lived approximately 500 years before Jesus and at that point in biblical history, Jerusalem had been ransacked. Most of the Jews had been exiled to Babylon. Following seventy years of captivity, a remnant of the Jews returned to the city and began to rebuild the Temple. After beginning well, however, the building work stalled. God gave both Zechariah and Haggai, another prophet, the job of encouraging the returning Jews to continue building. Zechariah's prophetic utterances were far-reaching, and they foretold not only Christ's first coming as Saviour but also His return to earth at the end of the age.

Zechariah for today

Much can be gleaned from this period in Jewish history that is relevant to Christian men and women today whose lives are linked in some way with the subject of homosexuality. One only has to read the books of Ezra and Nehemiah to learn the variety of ways in which God's work can be challenged and thwarted. In Ezra we read that after laying down the Temple foundation, the recent Jewish settlers were approached by people who had been living in the region for a number of years following the Assyrian victories. These people were a mixture of poor Jews who had been left behind and foreigners who had been relocated to the region. By the time the exiles returned to Jerusalem, the local people had assimilated their various faiths and settled upon a belief system, *the* God plus other gods, which was acceptable to all.

At first the current inhabitants, citing a shared worship of God, offered to work alongside the returning exiles and help build the Temple. After this offer of help was refused, the residents began to discourage the workers. They created an element of fear in the people by hiring counsellors or officials to work against the exiles (Ezra 4:5).

New or young believers with SSA issues can face similar challenges today. Their foundation is in Christ and their desire is to stop any sexual activity they are engaged in and/or address the temptations and struggles they have with same gender attraction. Most mainline denominations have a gay-friendly branch that will welcome and seek to help the new believer accommodate both their faith and their homosexuality. Coupled with the new laws and general positivity towards all things gay so prevalent in society it is extremely challenging for the new or young believer to remain strong in foundational truth.

Financial threats

Back in the time of Zechariah we read that this official opposition to the building work was both long-term and persistent in nature. Realizing that this approach was not breaking the exiles' resolve, the residents of that area finally wrote a letter to the new ruler stating that if he allowed the Jews to continue building the city, two things would happen: he would experience severe financial loss and he would no longer have direct influence in the Trans-Euphrates region. There's nothing like a threat to one's fiscal and power base to focus the mind!

Christian ministries that seek to serve believers struggling with all kinds of sexual brokenness have always been "Cinderella"-type ministries struggling to make financial ends meet while ministering to some of the neediest in any church congregation. On top of that there are now measures being drafted – or in some places already implemented – to make it illegal to offer counsel to those seeking help with their attraction, orientation, and/or behaviours.

Derision

Church-based Christianity is going through a rough patch and is often the butt of many satirical jokes through all forms of the media. The challenge is even greater for those addressing their homosexual inclinations when their efforts are met with societal contempt. This echoes what we see in the book of Nehemiah when we read that Sanballat and Tobiah, influential local men, were disturbed simply by the arrival of Nehemiah in Jerusalem (Nehemiah 2:10). They began to mock the Jewish plans to rebuild the city (Nehemiah 2:19). Ignoring their taunts, the exiles began their work and, with excellent planning and teamwork, much progress was made. But it resulted in further abuse:

> When Sanballat heard that we were rebuilding the wall, he became angry and was greatly incensed. He ridiculed the Jews, and in the presence of his associates and the army of Samaria, he said, "What are those feeble Jews doing? Will they restore their wall? Will they offer sacrifices? Will they finish in a day? Can they bring the stones back to life from those heaps of rubble – burned as they are?"
>
> Nehemiah 4:1–2

The returning Jews were not only accosted by those who were not their own, but were also ill-treated by the rich Jews who demanded extortionate interest on loans given to the poor who were desperately trying to provide their family with food (Nehemiah 5). Quite simply, those Jews who left the relative comfort of Babylon in order to re-establish God's Temple in God's city were confronted with anger, hostility, discouragement, and pressure – from both without and within.

God's Word tells us that we are all temples of the Holy Spirit (1 Corinthians 6:19) and we are being moulded and shaped and reworked in the best image of Jesus Christ Himself. Parts of our life have been, or still are, little more than piles of burned rubble. Rest assured, irrespective of how you feel today, my friend, none of it is wasted in God's economy.

So when I hear or read people's personal journey away from and sometimes back towards a life of homosexuality or other forms of sexual brokenness, it is easy to see how doubt, discouragement or outright opposition has gradually ground down even the most committed believers. The Bible encourages us to be not only as innocent as doves but *also* as wise as serpents (Matthew 10:16). Seeking to live a life pleasing to God will always incite opposition and, therefore, we need to ensure that we are fit for the purpose.

Encouragement

Before we start looking at ways to make ourselves fit for purpose I want to encourage you again with the words from Zechariah:

> As for you, because of the blood of my covenant with you,
> I will free your prisoners from the waterless pit.
> Return to your fortress, you prisoners of hope;
> even now I announce that I will restore twice as much
> to you.
>
> Zechariah 9:11–12

Although Zechariah was probably referring to the blood of the covenant of Moses in Exodus 24:1–8, we can read it as the blood of Christ that ushered in the new covenant thus bringing the repentant new life in Jesus. We who were once slaves to sin are now slaves to righteousness and filled with the hope that is in Christ. He alone is our fortress, our stronghold, and our tall tower. Therefore, we can leave behind our fleshly ways of coping and rely on Him alone to fulfil our needs. That promise is for now and for all eternity.

The one-degree Christian

Years ago, when I was a student of physical education, I chose to major in outdoor pursuits for my third year of study. Along with such usual activities as rock climbing, sailing, and caving, we all had to learn how to use a map and compass. I always lacked concentration when it came to the theoretical part of any subject so, instead of concentrating on the task in hand, I was too busy flipping open the lid, turning the housing from right to left and insisting that Scottie "beam me up" immediately.

That behaviour may have amused my eleven classmates down at base camp, but it did little to help me some 1,085 metres later on the fog-enshrouded summit of Mount Snowdon! There were no landmarks from which I could take my bearings and I required the very skill I had supposedly learned only hours earlier. I looked busy enough lining up points A and B on the map and, without moving the base plate, I turned the compass housing until the orienteering arrow pointed to the top of the map and stood up confident in my calculations. "On the count of three," shouted the instructor, "point in the direction of the base camp." On three I confidently thrust my right arm out to the side while the other eleven students pointed emphatically to their left.

In failing to take note of the direction-of-travel arrow, I had committed a classic schoolgirl error, thus ensuring that I was a full 180° off in my calculations. Fortunately, I humbled myself and, bowing to superior numbers, withdrew my right arm and quietly followed the other eleven down the mountain to safety.

Being 180° wrong is an obvious mistake and can be easily rectified. But some problems arise at a later point on a hike simply because the error was not at all obvious at the beginning of the journey. When in the great outdoors one always needs to be aware that there are two norths – magnetic north and true north – and they need to be taken into account when a hiker is embarking on a journey of some distance.

Awareness of the two norths is not necessary if the distance is inconsequential. For instance, if my destination (point B) is only 100 metres away from my starting point (point A), and is in full view at all times, it doesn't really matter if I have forgotten to allow for the difference between magnetic north and true north[43] because there is only a short distance to travel. However, if my point B is 10 km away from my starting point A, and I have not factored in the magnetic and true north discrepancy, then I shall be 464 metres (over a quarter of a mile to the non-metric) to one side of my intended destination.[44]

But what has this illustration got to do with the subject of this book?

A two-pronged tactic

Over the past few years I have noticed a disturbingly vocal increase in the general questioning and undermining of Christian men and women who have chosen to stand in their belief that sexual activity between members of the same sex is wrong. Coupled with this inquisitorial stance toward the

43 The difference changes every year; in the UK in 2014 the difference was 2° 40′ (http://www.geomag.bgs.ac.uk/data_service/models_compass/gma_calc.html).
44 Thanks to Alison John, a dear friend who happens to be a first-rate mathematician, for this calculation. Apparently, one divides the angle in half, finding its sine, and multiplying that by 10 km (or 10,000 metres). When you double the answer you then know the distance you are from your desired location.

individual, the traditional biblical exegesis itself is being pummelled from a number of directions. We should not be surprised at this two-pronged ploy by the enemy considering the first question in the Bible was the serpent asking Eve, "Did God really say, 'You must not eat from any tree in the garden'?" (Genesis 3:1). Now, in the twenty-first century, not only is the question as blatant as "Did God say?", but there is a more subtle follow-up question: "Is what God said still relevant for today?" Like an annoying drip, drip, drip from a leaky tap, there is a tendency to undermine God's Word with seemingly wise but definitely erroneous comments. These come from certain Christians whose concerns are about the need to be socially aware and relevant for today's individualistic approach to life.

Out of their compassion, these advocates for "relevancy" may well have walked for years with one or more individuals who seek resolution to their same-sex conflict. They have witnessed the pain and difficulties that often accompany such efforts. In an attempt to relieve the apparent unfairness of it all it is tempting for those who are preachers, teachers, or otherwise influential people to remove one of the barriers (the interpretation of biblical intent) and offer a more inclusive church in which all people can be themselves before Christ.

Since this kind of church seems birthed in love and compassion, it seems harsh to argue against such efforts to ensure that people feel both welcomed and accepted. And yet, this ill-founded love and compassion is actually the compass illustration come to life. If a hiker chooses to ignore the difference between map grid north and magnetic north that is clearly written in the bottom corner of every map, he or she may walk for 10 km in an easterly direction but because of the approximate 2° deviation between the two norths, that hiker will never reach their intended destination.

The Metropolitan Community Churches in the United Kingdom's online portal[45] illustrates the point I am trying to make. The MCCs are gay-affirming churches and are found in a number of countries throughout the world. They fully affirm the orthodox theological stance cited in both the Apostles' Creed and the Nicene Creed, and would stand with much of what is taught and what happens in a traditional evangelical church. All is well until we read further on their website:

> What influences lead us to new ways of understanding Scripture? New scientific information, social changes, and personal experience are perhaps the greatest forces for change in the way we interpret the Bible and develop our beliefs.[46]

In this Christian church there are three areas that are stated above Scripture: alleged scientific findings, changing attitudes in society, and the increased importance being placed on the personal story. The MCC is not 180° out and walking in the wrong direction, but the compass reading is sufficiently inaccurate as to jeopardize its reaching the desired destination. To ensure we stand firm in the truth and remain standing firm in the truth, it is necessary for us to create something I have called the "framework of truth".

The framework of truth

> One of them, an expert in the law, tested him with this question: "Teacher, which is the greatest commandment in the Law?" Jesus replied: "'Love the Lord your God with all your heart and with all your soul and with all

45   See https://sites.google.com/site/frbraunston/home.
46   https://sites.google.com/site/frbraunston/thebibleandsexuality.

your mind.'This is the first and greatest commandment. And the second is like it: 'Love your neighbour as yourself.'All the Law and the Prophets hang on these two commandments."

Matthew 22:35–40

If your vertical relationship is sound, says Jesus, then your horizontal relationships – loving your neighbour as yourself – will be sound. I believe the mess many Christians and Christian ministries are in today is due to the fact that they have tried to fulfil the second commandment, while allowing the first commandment to fall into disarray.

Trying to love other people without God's backbone of truth, righteousness, love, and mercy will adversely affect our actions. They are no longer pure, but are tainted, because we have knocked God out of first place and put our feelings and other people into the primary position. This taints our ministry opportunities to other believers, outreach activities toward those who don't yet know the Lord, friendships inside and outside the community of believers, and interaction with the world in general. When the second commandment precedes the first, then we merely love and serve as the world loves and serves, and that exposes us to the hidden force of relativism.

But if I am committed to obeying primarily the first commandment then I, by default, am committed to surrendering all of my loves, my desires, my thoughts, and my behaviours to God. Aligning my heart, soul, and mind to the truth of God minimizes the danger of me engaging incorrectly in my horizontal relationships. Without God's strong backbone of truth at the core, individuals and ministries and church denominations will flip-flop and lean toward expressions of love that may be acceptable in a godless world, but do not rightfully represent God's standard of love. But how do we ensure that we don't fall into this trap?

It can be tempting and all too easy to create a god that is similar to God, but leave out the bits that we find either difficult to understand or hard to follow. In the end we will create something that incorporates all of our individual best bits but also someone who is just that bit bigger and more powerful than ourselves. In truth, all that we have created is a mere *super me*. Not surprisingly God has a more accurate view of Himself: "I am the Lord, your Holy One, Israel's Creator, your King" (Isaiah 43:15).

Seeing ourselves as God sees us

Standing in the framework of truth is all about choosing to love God with all of our heart, soul, and mind – even if the sin-ridden world into which we are born, and the variety of circumstances we have encountered growing up, may challenge our chosen position. However, choosing to see ourselves as God sees us is imperative if we are to succeed. As men and women who may well have issues around their gender and same-sex attraction, there are two Scriptures that are worth ingesting and declaring as truth:

> So God created mankind in his own image, in the image of God he created them; male and female he created them.
>
> **Genesis 1:27**

> As a father has compassion on his children, so the Lord has compassion on those who fear him; for he knows how we are formed, he remembers that we are dust.
>
> **Psalm 103:13–14**

Our own brokenness, plus the input of and interaction with others, distorts the truth of who we really are. Only God sees us perfectly and He declares that we are fearfully and wonderfully made (Psalm 139:15). This does not mean the sin and brokenness are part of His perfect design; they are what mar His intent, but they do not remove it.

Wage war against untruth

So, what are we to do? How do we move beyond acknowledgment and into application? We remove anything or anyone that interferes with the primacy of this relationship. With Satan, the world, and our flesh wanting us to deviate from God's best, this is no easy task. It requires lifelong application if we are truly to remain submitted to God. Paul understands the dilemma:

> "I have the right to do anything," you say – but
> not everything is beneficial. "I have the right to do
> anything" – but I will not be mastered by anything.
>
> 1 Corinthians 6:12

Again, this framework of truth has nothing to do with my thoughts, feelings, attractions, or desires, but simply to do with the truth. It is like creating a timber frame at the beginning of a house build: the outline of the house may be apparent at the end of a working day, but without walls, floors, or a roof in sight, the owner is unlikely to be moving in and calling it home! It is, however, a very good beginning.

The build begins

Once the framework of truth is in place, building a house of substance can then begin. I have chosen to see God as He is, to see myself as God sees me, and to remove any thought/

attitude/behaviour that contradicts what God states. This means that as I address various areas of sexual brokenness, I ensure first and foremost that they come within this vertical framework of truth.

Very early on in my Christian walk, I had to address the area of gender identity. A description of what I did is given in my first book, *Out of Egypt*.[47] But, suffice to say, I had to keep gender identity in the framework of truth and choose to believe it as truth for a long period of time before I was *emotionally* in agreement with God. When tempted to stray outside of these boundaries, I had to ask and answer some basic questions:

- Who is right? God or me?
- Does God have His best for me even if this is hard?
- What does God say in His Word and am I living according to that truth?

That process kept me in a good vertical relationship with God. And, although I didn't feel any different, I chose to *imprison* myself in this framework of truth, knowing that the structure was sound and that the floors, walls, and roof were being created. It was two-and-a-half years after I had first brought my problems with gender identity to the Lord that I experienced an emotional breakthrough, but the revelatory truth that I am a woman took root and has flourished from that time and has never been an issue since.

A door to intimacy

Discipleship isn't easy but it does offer great reward. The more we view life as God views life that vertical relationship with Him, and in Him, strengthens and matures. And when we take

47   Jeanette Howard, *Out of Egypt: Leaving Lesbianism Behind*, Oxford: Monarch Books, 1991.

sides with God and make His attitude toward sin our attitude toward sin, we continue to reinforce the structure, thus allowing God to start creating *our home*. Is it too much to hope that as we live within this God-defined vertical structure we can walk arm in arm with Him as Enoch did, or speak face to face as Moses once did? All I know is that Psalm 25:14 states: "The Lord confides in those who fear him; he makes his covenant known to them."

Consciously bringing our lives within this vertical structure can't help but change us. We find that spending time in His presence and pursuing intimacy with God is no longer considered a distraction to our everyday living, but as *foundational* to all that we do. We look forward to reading His Word and waiting on Him. We come to realize that the *outcome* of our relationship with Him is secondary to our relationship with Him. It is that realization which enables us to fulfil the second commandment of loving our neighbour with God's love.

Intimacy offers protection

Temptation comes in many forms and in varying degrees of strength. One of my greatest weaknesses over the years has been to become enmeshed in dependent relationships. I was unaware of the practical implications of not living under the mandate of the greatest commandment by loving the Lord with my whole heart, soul, and mind. That lack weakened my ability to engage and interact with others in a godly way. Instead of coming from that vertically secure place of relative wholeness, I would try and engage the horizontal – the loving my neighbour – from my own rather damaged situation that was also positioned on the horizontal plane. Instead of having my fundamental dependency firmly entrenched in the Lord and thus operating from a certain level of security, I entered into friendships that unwittingly demanded that some poor soul meet all of my long-held and near primal needs. It would be safe to say that I entered into friendships and relationships with armfuls of baggage rather than boxes of gifts!

I described the vertical structure as a place of relative wholeness not because there is anything faulty in the *God-down* direction of this relationship, but because I have yet to grasp, and will never this side of eternity, the enormous ramifications of having the Lord make His home in and with me (John 14:23).

Intimacy offers hope

Lining up one's life under this one single command may seem not only extremely daunting, but also rather unappealing. And it is. At least it is unappealing to the flesh because it puts restrictions on the natural wayward self that likes to self-determine and pursue its own interpretation of freedom. The flesh will never want to come under the jurisdiction of God and we would be foolish to expect that to change (Romans 8:7), which is why the Holy Spirit works in our spirit to want to do something, and then enables us to carry out that desire (Philippians 2:13).

Dr Who is a British television programme that recently celebrated its fiftieth anniversary. It attracts a cult-like following all over the world. I actually remember the first show back in the days of black and white television, when the studio sets were made out of little more than cardboard boxes that would skid along the shiny floor as the actors jumped on them in their bid to escape from some fierce and dangerous alien. Dr Who is a Time Lord who travels through space in a machine that looks like, from the outside at least, nothing more than a police telephone box common on British streets since the early 1920s. The design of the police box changed frequently during the subsequent decades and the one now made famous by the celebrated Time Lord was in production during the late 1950s and early 1960s. Standing about two metres tall and little more than a metre square, this blue box seems incapable of housing a burly policeman, let alone the workings of a time machine. But this box has a secret: the inside is bigger than the outside and, once through the narrow door, the TARDIS[48] reveals its true multi-levelled size.

I don't want to sound blasphemous, but one can equate that box to the framework of truth I have previously described. To an untrained eye, God's way seems terribly constricted and bent on denying freedom. But the truth is that God's way frees us from the constraints of our sinful disposition. It opens us up to life in abundance. Endeavouring to love God with our *whole* heart, soul, and mind not only sets our feet on firm ground (Psalm 40), but also enables us to walk in spacious places (Psalms 118:5; 18:19). From that position of strength and protection, I can then seek to fulfil God's second great commandment – that of loving, serving, and ministering to my neighbour.

Happy ever after?

It would be naive to think that this framework of truth guarantees a problem-free life, for we are not yet in our resurrected bodies and dwelling on the new earth. However, we make ourselves a prisoner of hope – not by placing our hope in a favourable outcome such as orientational change, marriage, children, or anything else, but by putting our faith in the person of Jesus Christ. *The Message* translates the Zechariah passage as follows:

> And you, because of my blood covenant with you,
> I'll release your prisoners from their hopeless cells.
> Come home, hope-filled prisoners!

48   As a Whovian, I do feel obligated to explain for the uninitiated the acronym TARDIS: Time and Relative Dimension in Space.

This very day I'm declaring a double bonus –
everything you lost returned twice-over!

Zechariah 9:11–12

Being *at home* – that is, dwelling in the presence and power of God – enables each one of us to live a life pleasing to the Lord and useful to His purposes.

In a large house there are articles not only of gold and silver, but also of wood and clay; some are for special purposes and some for common use. Those who cleanse themselves from the latter will be instruments for special purposes, made holy, useful to the Master and prepared to do any good work.

2 Timothy 2:20–21

During the course of this book, we will look at some of the ways we can strengthen ourselves in the Lord and help others in their faith-filled journey. Do not be discouraged if you have been living out of the second commandment – the horizontal – and have taken your eyes off the first commandment – the vertical – resulting in difficulties in attitudes or relationships. All is not lost. Come before the Lord. Talk to Him about this reversal of priority. Make confession where appropriate. Commit to living according to His sense of importance, and then I encourage you to take this verse from the apostle Paul and make it your own:

May the God of hope fill you with all joy and peace as you trust in him, so that you may overflow with hope by the power of the Holy Spirit.

Romans 15:13

Chapter 5

Who are You?

> I am not my sin. I am not my temptation to
> sin. By the blood of Jesus Christ, I have been
> liberated from this bondage. I will have all sorts of
> identities, to be sure, especially in our crazily over-
> psychoanalytic age. But at the very least, none of
> these identities should be essentially defined by my
> attraction to that which separates me from God.[49]
>
> Mark A. Yarhouse, *Understanding Sexual Identity*

Who do you think you are? Depending on your biblical knowledge, you may be able to quote a string of "correct" Scriptures, all affirming your position in Christ and relationship with God the Father. Head knowledge of the truth is, of course, only part of the story. It is what we have allowed to filter down into our hearts that determines the quality of our relationship with God. Oftentimes, He will lovingly point out a false thought or belief that is doing its best to sabotage our Christian journey, and will encourage us to release that particular burden. Dwelling in the framework of truth automatically challenges any wrong and potentially damaging thoughts a person may be entertaining, even unwittingly, and enables the Holy Spirit's transformative work to continue.

> Don't become so well-adjusted to your culture that
> you fit into it without even thinking. Instead, fix your
> attention on God. You'll be changed from the inside
> out. Readily recognize what he wants from you, and

49   Michael W. Hannon, "Against Heterosexuality", *First Things*, March 2014 (http://www.firstthings.com/article/2014/03/against-heterosexuality).

quickly respond to it. Unlike the culture around you,
always dragging you down to its level of immaturity,
God brings the best out of you, develops well-formed
maturity in you.

Romans 12:2, *The Message*

In my many years of Christian involvement in the subject of
homosexuality, I have noticed that it is not necessarily the men
and women who experience a change in attraction or sexual
desire that go on to live satisfying Christian lives. Instead, it is
the men and women who are able to cast off their *identification*
with sinful thoughts and practices that are best able to embrace
the newness and potential of a life in Christ.

What I am not

I am not a sinner saved by grace. I certainly *was* someone who
was estranged from God because of my sin and rebellious ways
but, thanks to Christ's substitutionary act on the cross and His
subsequent resurrection from the dead, I am now reconciled
with the Father and seeking to live under the guidance and
empowerment of Christ's Spirit living in me. I have been born
from on high and have completely new DNA, God's DNA,
residing in me and flowing through me. I am no longer a sinner
but a saint. I am a daughter of the King and I am seated in the
heavenly realms enjoying the blessings and benefits of being a
co-heir along with my beloved Lord Jesus.

Does this mean that I no longer sin? Sadly not. It is my
desire to live a life fully pleasing to the Lord, but I still have
thoughts, attitudes, and behaviours that are incongruent with
my royal status. I am a cherished child of the King, but I do
not always live in accordance with that truth and will always
need His grace to empower me to live in truth. Bill Johnson,

the senior pastor of Bethel Church in Redding, California, used to have the following as a tag line on his website: "I cannot afford to have a thought in my head that is not in His." How true.

Men and women addressing issues surrounding their same-sex attraction often have to deal with one or both of the following damaged identities: sexual identity and gender identity. We will look at both of these in more detail later in the book. But first, I want to explore the truth of who we are in order to look at our damaged areas from a place of strength. Before the technological age, bank tellers were trained to spot counterfeit bank notes – not by looking at previous attempts at forgery, but by spending time handling and getting to know every detail of the genuine article. Familiarizing themselves with the real currency enabled them to spot a phoney with greater ease.

Chosen and appointed

Back in 1984, having spent a year teaching at a Christian-based boarding school in Australia, I left the country owning a Bible and with an interest in Christianity. But I was not yet in possession of salvation faith. I didn't know any Christians in England who resembled those I had met during the last two months of my time abroad. So, left with just a Bible for company, I began to read. One month later I read John 15:16: "You did not choose me, but I chose you and appointed you to go and bear fruit – fruit that will last."

The verse blew me away. The realization that I was already chosen by Jesus and all I had to do was respond to Him and accept His overtures of love was potentially a life-changing moment. Of course, it wasn't that simple. I knew in my spirit that if I accepted Christ as my Lord and Saviour, I had to turn my back on my lesbian behaviour and the only way of thinking I had ever known – all this for a man I couldn't even see!

Two significant things happened as I surrendered my life to Christ. The first was that I experienced the most excruciating physical pain in my chest followed by a large hand that ministered warmth and healing. Then the Holy Spirit gave me a picture of the lower part of a woman, wearing a skirt and court shoes, standing on a stage talking. I had no idea who the person was or what the person was talking about. "Who's that?" I asked, confused by the film being played before me. "That's you," I was told, "and you're talking about Me."

A blessing and a dilemma

Over the years, this Scripture and the accompanying picture have been both a blessing and a dilemma. The verses have blessed me, especially during the very hard early years of continued same-sex attraction and temptations. I needed to remember that Jesus had chosen me in the *midst* of my sin and was not, therefore, going to abandon me as I sought to leave it all behind. The combination of the Scripture and the picture, however, often created certain confusion in me when considering work options. What exactly did the phrase "appointed you to go and bear fruit – fruit that will last" actually mean? Was it to do with character building, good deeds, making converts, or a glorious mixture of all three including, perhaps, some other factor I had yet to discover? If it was to do with character building, then I already had plenty of character, which was, of course, half of my problem! The characteristics that seemed to come readily to the fore were usually on the list of those belonging to my sinful nature rather than those resulting from being led by the Spirit.

If "bearing fruit" was to do with good deeds, then I can't say that mine really lasted. I was very good in crisis moments but pretty useless at long-term commitment. And if "fruit" referred to the task of making converts, then I can assure you I was no Billy Graham in the making. Indeed, in my thirty years as a Christian, I have only ever knowingly led one person to the Lord and that is because a friend brought this lady to say the sinner's prayer with me, having taken pity on my poor track record!

Labouring under partial understanding

I don't think I was alone in my confusion for I am sure many Christians labour under a false or only partial understanding of the term "fruit". When they read in Matthew, "by their fruit you will recognize them" (Matthew 7:16), some people are gripped by fear in case the good deeds they are producing are not up to God's standard and will fail His quality control. A number of men and women struggling with SSA often fail to keep the verse in context. They start worrying about their own Christian life with all of its wayward desires and temptations that no one else *appears* to experience, and thus conclude that their life falls far short of their interpretation of God's expectations. Their fears couldn't be further from the truth and, as we shall see later on, it is their heroic steadfastness in the midst of difficulties that produces *fine* Kingdom fruit.

While the John 15:16 verse was pertinent to my particular salvation story, it contains truth for us all. In 2 Thessalonians 2:13b–14, the apostle Paul writes:

> God picked you out as his from the very start. Think
> of it: included in God's original plan of salvation by
> the bond of faith in the living truth. This is the life of

the Spirit he invited you to through the Message we delivered, in which you get in on the glory of our Master, Jesus Christ.

The Message

Irrespective of how you feel right now, the truth is that God chose you to be in full relationship with Him from the beginning. He called each believer to enjoy the richness of life that comes from a bond that is birthed in love and maintained by His divine nature.

I am the true vine, and my Father is the gardener. He cuts off every branch in me that bears no fruit, while every branch that does bear fruit he prunes so that it will be even more fruitful. You are already clean because of the word I have spoken to you. Remain in me, and I will remain in you. No branch can bear fruit by itself; it must remain in the vine. Neither can you bear fruit unless you remain in me. I am the vine; you are the branches. If a man remains in me and I in him, he will bear much fruit; apart from me you can do nothing. If anyone does not remain in me, he is like a branch that is thrown away and withers; such branches are picked up, thrown into the fire and burned. If you remain in me and my words remain in you, ask whatever you wish, and it will be given you. This is to my Father's glory, that you bear much fruit, showing yourselves to be my disciples. As the Father has loved me, so have I loved you. Now remain in my love. If you obey my commands, you will remain in my love, just as I have obeyed my Father's commands and remain in his love. I have told you this so that my joy may be in you and that your joy may be complete.

John 15:1–11

"Remain in Me"

The best way we can ensure that our identity is truly God-given is to remain in Christ. Jesus says this: "I am the vine; you are the branches. If a man remains in me and I in him, he will bear much fruit; apart from me you can do nothing" (John 15:5).

"Apart from me," says Jesus, "you can do nothing." How many of us at one time or another have been guilty of chasing round, trying to produce our own fruit? We have sought help and healing through friends and pastors, via books or DVDs, at conferences or at the feet of persuasive speakers. We have prayed and fasted, confessed and re-committed. We have been accountable until we are blue in the face.

Our motives will have been exemplary and our commitment incomparable, but so often our planning and efforts have proved earthbound and man-made. How many of us make the mistake of recognizing our need, but end up asking God only to bless our efforts rather than lead the way? Is it any wonder that so many brothers and sisters become exhausted by their efforts to change, become spiritually dry, and then, as the Beyond Ex-Gay survey seems to show, end up packing it all in?

Clinging to the cross, abiding in the vine

At some point, as a non-Christian on the verge of salvation, I became suddenly aware of the importance of the cross. From being a mere lump of wood on which some man allegedly died for my sins, the Holy Spirit miraculously unveiled the truth of the crucifixion and its eternal significance in my life. From merely nodding my head in acknowledgment of some historical event, I finally realized the truth that it is the *only hope* for the salvation of my soul and reconciliation with God.

A new convert clings to the base of the cross, grateful for the gift of life and yet fearful of letting go in case they wander too far from God's life-giving grace. So far so good, but I believe that as a Christian matures he or she must grasp the significance of another piece of wood – the vine – if they are to receive the fullness that is theirs in Christ. Just as a new believer clings *to* the truth of the cross and Jesus' subsequent resurrection as the means for new life, the maturing Christian should hold fast *in* the vine in order to receive all that is necessary for life in abundance (John 10:10). How is this done?

Grafting, not clinging

I spent many years living slightly inland in an area of England that is becoming quite renowned for its wine industry. Because of the climate it will never rival the Napa Valley in California or the Western Cape in South Africa for output, but in recent years a type of grape has been developed especially for the English growing conditions and is now producing a reasonable quantity of very palatable wine. I have often walked footpaths that run parallel to the vineyards and have observed these vines during the course of a year. I watch the changes that take place. From the stark outline set against a low wintry sun, to the first flowers bursting open in May, the rampant growth of leaf and grape over the summer months, and the marvellous rich colours in September and October signalling the time of harvest – these have always reminded me that the Father is "the vinedresser" (John 1:1, NASB).

Studying the grafting of vines can teach us much about our own Christian walk. Field grafting, the attaching of a new strain of fruit onto an established vine, is quite common in wine-producing vineyards, as it allows for a change in the variety of fruit without going to the expense of replanting the whole field. There is, however, some loss to production because of the grafting process, but this is only the loss of one year's crop. Compare that to the loss of years of yield experienced if new immature vines are planted and the vinedresser must wait for them to mature. During the dormant winter period, the vine grower carefully chooses the disease-free implant or scion, as it is known professionally, of his desired new grape variety and the grafting process begins in April.

Not surprisingly, teams of skilled grafters are required for this job, as no goodness will pass from the vine into the potential branch unless both the vine and the scions are cut correctly. After cutting the mature rootstock, the tapered scion is inserted into the cut at the correct angle to maximize as much bare wood contact as possible. The joint is then taped and all remaining bare wood is sealed for protection. Timely cuts into the base of the rootstock over the next year allow the vine to bleed. This ensures the scion isn't receiving too much sap from the rootstock, which would force the scion to pop out of its graft. If all goes well, a new two-variety grapevine is created; the original vine continues at the root system and lower trunk, while the new variety becomes the upper trunk and the *fruiting portion* of the vine.

The source

Jesus states categorically: "I am the vine, you are the branches", thus reminding us of our power base being in Him, in the natural order of things. God is the source of all good things and we are the *recipients* of His blessing. There is no ambiguity in this passage. The Bible makes it clear that if we fail to remain in Christ we are "like a branch that is thrown away and withers" (John 15:6a). We cannot underestimate the importance of this excerpt: without the vine there are no branches and without the branches there is no fruit.

In the book of Hosea, after promising Israel forgiveness and restoration, God states: "your fruitfulness comes from me" (Hosea 14:8). And the same is true for us today. If we remain in Christ, we cannot help but be fruitful, for it is His goodness, His love, and His power coursing through our body. The new heart and spirit we received at salvation is strengthened and empowered as we surrender to His ways. As we continue to submit and *remain* in Him, we can confidently stand alongside the apostle Paul and declare that "in him we live and move and have our being" (Acts 17:28).

The pruning

The Bible states that "every branch that does bear fruit He [the Father] prunes" (John 15:2b). Reading up on vine management can give the Christian much food for thought as we learn that pruning removes the woody growth of the past season and sets the vine up for the coming cycle. Even at this stage, in the dormant winter period when it appears that nothing is happening, the coming season's yield is being established as the vine grower prunes each branch.

It is worth noting that well-pruned vines will, in northern Europe, produce twenty to thirty bunches of grapes each weighing around 1kg. Interestingly, an unpruned vine may also produce fruit, but it is of a much poorer quality than the fruit from a pruned vine. And, although the yield remains quite high on an unpruned vine, the grape itself becomes smaller every subsequent season. Not only that but, because grapes grow on new wood, the yield from an unpruned vine becomes gradually more inaccessible as the old wood gets in the way of the new yield. Timely pruning by the grower ensures the best yield year on year; therefore, if we want to produce good fruit we must *welcome* and not avoid God's pruning saw!

Feeding

It requires a lot of energy to produce fruit. A good grower will have already planted the vine in the most favourable position regarding sunlight and shelter from extreme weather. But the soil also needs to be nutritious for the vine to be at its most productive. The plant requires a good balance of nitrogen, potassium, magnesium phosphorous, plus a number of lesser nutrients, if it is to thrive and bear fruit.

And that is no different to us. Standing firm in our commitment to Christ irrespective of the struggles and temptations we may be facing requires us to be well fed. The passage in the book of John continues: "If… my words remain in you…" – if we feed on God's Word daily, we will be nourished. This feeding does not mean relying solely on Bible reading notes, but feasting on and digesting large chunks of the Bible. (I am *not* against Bible reading notes per se, but I do see them rather as a snack and as an addition to rather than a replacement for concentrated Bible reading.) From the early chapters in Genesis, we read of God's intended relationship with His creation, and the rest of the book continues to express God's love for and commitment to us. Knowing the truth of who we are sets us free from the lies that we have come to believe through our own brokenness, the brokenness of others, and this world that seeks to separate us from the reality that is found in God.

Is your graft clean and secure and receiving every bit of goodness from the True Vine? Or has the joint been damaged in any way, allowing some disease to infect the connection? Are you well fed or malnourished?

The benefits of abiding in Christ

Quite simply, the benefits of abiding in Christ will mean that His "sap" will provide all the nourishment we need for quality fruit to grow. And what will that fruit be? We find the fruit listed in Galatians 5:22 as that of love, peace, patience, kindness, goodness, faithfulness, gentleness, self-control, and of course that much needed fruit of joy. The more we can *remain* embedded in Christ, the more our whole life will be transformed because our thoughts and actions and ability to cope will be prompted by our relationship with Him. One of the most awe-inspiring truths that should encourage every Christian is the knowledge that our abiding in Christ brings glory to God (John 15:8). The mystery to me is that God, who is fully glorious in His own right, considers my abiding in His Son as a way of bringing *more* glory to Him! The apostle Paul writes in Corinthians:

> But thanks be to God, who always leads us in triumphal procession in Christ and through us spreads everywhere the fragrance of the knowledge of him. *For we are to God the aroma of Christ* among those who are being saved and those who are perishing.
>
> **2 Corinthians 2:14–15, emphasis mine**

Not only does God consider our abiding as an act that brings Him further glory, but also our personal fragrance is, to God, *exactly the same* as that of His beloved Jesus. To God there is no difference between us! Importantly, the strength of this scent is not dependent on how much is put on us, but on how much emerges from within. As we become more Christ-like, His fragrance will ooze from every pore in our body and our very lives will evidence the reality that Jesus is alive today, thus bringing God glory. And why has Jesus taken time to teach us the analogy of the vine? "I have told you this so that my joy may be in you and that your joy may be complete" (John 15:11).

Confident that our graft into Christ, the vine, is secure and protected we can derive joy from being in Christ, irrespective of circumstances. Over the years, I have experienced a number of people being quite angry on my behalf. "It's not fair," they tell me, "that God makes you gay and then tells you that you can't do anything about it. Surely He wants you to be happy?" It often pans out that the individual is not railing against my situation at all, but that some part of my story has highlighted an element in their own personal Christian walk that God may be challenging them to lay down.

Whether we like it or not, Christian and non-Christian people alike will not only scrutinize how we address our personal walk away from homosexuality, but may also use our journey as an opportunity to put the whole of the Christian faith on trial! They will want to know that what we say and believe in actually has relevance when "the rubber hits the road". A well-grafted branch that sources its energy from the mature rootstock will bear much quality fruit. And even during the difficult times, that branch will bear fruit of love, joy, peace, patience, kindness, goodness, faithfulness, gentleness, and self-control. The Bible is full of similar encouraging imagery.

But blessed is the one who trusts in the Lord, whose confidence is in him. They will be like a tree planted by the water that sends out its roots by the stream. It does not fear when heat comes; its leaves are always green. It has no worries in a year of drought and never fails to bear fruit.

Jeremiah 17:7–8

To stand within the framework of truth, to love with our whole heart, soul, mind, and body, requires full submission to and dependence upon God. People in today's society scoff at such a position, dismissing it as a place of weakness that is to be avoided at all costs. But they do this without recognizing their own acquiescence to cultural demands and near total reliance on others to give them an identity and sense of self-worth.

However, we are created to be in a place of submission and dependence in order that we may be able to receive and operate from a place of power – God's power. This abiding occurs in the heart, which means that I can remain at rest even when challenged from thoughts within and stressors from without. Winds may blow and waters may rise, but the branch that remains fully grafted and receiving from the vine cannot help but produce fruit for others to feed on. In his book *Abide in Christ* the South African writer, teacher, and pastor Andrew Murray wrote this:

> Receive what you do not comprehend, submit to what you cannot understand, accept and expect what to reason appears a mystery, believe what looks impossible, walk in a way which you know not – such are the first lessons in the school of God.[50]

I wrote earlier that I believe wrong expectations have been a significant stumbling block to many brothers and sisters who have sought to bring their wayward sexuality under the Lordship of Christ. In the next couple of chapters we will look at the land the Israelites left behind in Egypt and the land they actually inherited. How good were their memories of their previous life? Did what they were promised match up to their expectations, and if not, what did they do with their disappointment?

50   Andrew Murray, *Abide in Christ*, Wilder, VA: Wilder Publications, 2008, Kindle edition, p. 136. Note that this classic devotional book was first published in 1888.

Chapter 6
Expectations, Wants, and Needs

I f I were to line up a class of twenty seven-year-olds and
give nineteen of them five sweets each but give the last
child in the line only one sweet, a loud and unrelenting cry
of "It's not fair!" would ring out from all of the pupils present.
The average seven- and eight-year-old would describe fairness
as meaning that everyone gets the same, irrespective of who
they are.

My parents were very keen that the four of us, two boys and
two girls, were treated in exactly the same way, as much as it
was possible. Despite our differences in age and interests, my
sister and I were often dressed identically and treated as one
unit. We were both members of the same swimming club and
attended weekly ballet lessons, had identical bicycles and we
were even given similar presents at Christmas. Around the age
of ten, I desperately wanted riding lessons and was prepared
to give up every other hobby and help around the house in
order to pursue this one love. My parents also wanted me to
learn to ride, but denied me the opportunity. They explained
that if they paid for me to ride, they would also have to pay for
everyone else, and that would cost far too much money. Indeed
it would have. However, the truth was that none of my siblings
wanted to ride and had – and still have to this day – absolutely
no interest in horses.

Yet my parents, until the day they died, never wavered from
this *reasoned* approach that fairness meant that we all received
five sweets whether we wanted them or not. Without doubt my
parents believed they were doing the right thing by treating us

all in the same way. I can only speak for myself, but I grew up feeling overlooked and uncared for and, quite honestly, felt quite unknown to my parents.

But if fairness isn't about everyone being treated in the same way and receiving equal portions then what is it? An expert in special needs education, Richard D. Lavoie, writes: "In actuality, the definition of fairness has little to do with treating people in an identical manner. The true definition of fairness is: 'Fairness means that everyone gets what he or she needs.'"[51] Lavoie goes on to say that he does not believe that fairness and equality are synonymous and that, in order to be fair, individuals must be treated differently depending on what they need and not what they want. For this to succeed, of course, the parents have to have the necessary tools to differentiate between the needs and wants of each individual child.

Ultimately, only God can do this perfectly. And that is precisely how He "parented" the people of Israel as He brought them out of Egypt and forged them into a nation.

God's promise

> The land you are entering to take over is not like the land of Egypt, from which you have come, where you planted your seed and irrigated it by foot as in a vegetable garden. But the land you are crossing the Jordan to take possession of is a land of mountains and valleys that drinks rain from heaven. It is a land the Lord your God cares for; the eyes of the Lord your God are continually on it from the beginning of the year to its end.
>
> **Deuteronomy 11:10–12**

---

51   Richard D. Lavoie, "Fairness: To each according to his needs" (http://www.ricklavoie.com/fairnessart.html).

The above statement from the book of Deuteronomy states quite clearly that God is not giving His people more of the same but without the Egyptian presence; God is saying that *every* aspect of the Promised Land is different, from the topography to the rule.

A radically different source

I'm not giving you a predominantly flat land, says the Lord, which is dependent on seasonal flooding and your hard work. I am not giving you a land that you can partially control while ignoring the arid higher terrain fit only for burial grounds. I am not giving you a land in which you are slaves to the elements, slaves to the citizens, and slaves to your own sinful nature. But I am giving you "*a land of mountains and valleys that drinks rain from heaven*" (Deuteronomy 11:10–11, emphasis mine).

God does not promise an easy land that stretches as far as the eye can see. There will be mountains and valleys, says the Lord, but I am present at the highest point and in the deepest depth, and every square metre of the land is known by Me. In Deuteronomy 11:13–15 God says:

> So if you faithfully obey the commands I am giving you
> today – to love the Lord your God and to serve him with
> all your heart and with all your soul – then I will send rain
> on your land in season, both autumn and spring rains,
> so that you may gather in your grain, new wine and oil.
> I will provide grass in the fields for your cattle, and you
> will eat and be satisfied.

For the Hebrew ex-slave, current nomad, and potential landowner, life in the Promised Land was going to be radically different because God is the source and provider of all things.

The garlic and the leeks that their parents had craved during the early part of the exodus had required great physical effort to grow. It involved transporting water by yoke or foot pump from the River Nile up to the high ground in order to grow their vegetables. But now, promised the Lord, life was going to be radically different.

Expectations

Moses had also told them:

> He will love you and bless you and increase your numbers. He will bless the fruit of your womb, the crops of your land – your grain, new wine and olive oil – the calves of your herds and the lambs of your flocks in the land he swore to your ancestors to give you. You will be blessed more than any other people; none of your men or women will be childless, nor will any of your livestock be without young. The Lord will keep you free from every disease. He will not inflict on you the horrible diseases you knew in Egypt, but he will inflict them on all who hate you.
>
> **Deuteronomy 7:13–15**

Living in the Promised Land seemed almost too good to be true. The assured blessings from God must have stirred such great expectations in the hearts of those men and women who had tramped through arid desert since childhood. At last they would find a home they could enjoy in which they could settle and flourish. Admittedly, they had to drive out the current inhabitants before the land could be fully theirs, but God had promised to drive the enemies out before them *and* deliver all the kings into their hands. How hard could it be?

Seven years after entering the land of Canaan, God's people were feeling pretty battered and, with the exception of the ever-chirpy Caleb, less enthused about God's gift to them. Without doubt the land was fertile and there were a great many riches, both man-made and natural, throughout the country. But the land's inhabitants had proved difficult to budge.

However, there had been sufficient times of victory during those years that, even though there was still work to be done and land to be taken, God deemed it right to allocate different portions to the different tribes. Some land east of the River Jordan had already been given to Reuben, Gad, and the half-tribe of Manasseh, and the Levites knew that they would not be receiving any land for an inheritance. Judah, Ephraim, and the other half-tribe of Manasseh knew that they were to receive the land Jacob had promised them some 450 years earlier (Genesis 48:22). Lots were drawn for the remaining tribes and the division of land fell as predicted earlier by both Jacob and Moses.

The land is not uniform

All of the land was the Promised Land given by God for the blessing of His people. But He did not stand the tribes in a row and give them the equivalent of five sweets all wrapped in the same paper and tasting exactly the same. The Israelites were chosen by God and were equally loved by Him, but each tribe inherited different elements of His overall promise so that, together, they inherited the complete place of blessing.

Fertile plains, lush foothills, mountainous regions, large fresh-water lakes, and a long coastline all offered the Israelites ample ways by which they could thrive in this new land. In order to enjoy God's provisions, all His people had to do was accept their given allocation, individually apply themselves to the task in hand, and adopt an attitude of thanksgiving towards their generous God. Unfortunately, not all of the Israelites rose to the occasion. One tribe in particular, the tribe of Dan, chose to go their own way with disastrous consequences.

We need to talk about Dan

What has the history of the Danite tribe got to do with bringing same-sex attractions under the Lordship of Christ? As we spend the rest of the chapter looking at this group of people and their response to God, it is my prayer that you will see that some of the choices facing men and women who are struggling with gay attraction and temptation are not that different from the choices facing the people of Dan.

Fig. 1

The land allocated to the tribe of Dan is clearly stated in Joshua 19:40–46 and can be viewed on the map (Fig. 1). On offer was the harbour of Joppa (now known as Jaffa) from which ran trade routes leading not only in a north–south direction, but also inland connecting them with the rest of Israel. Although Israel is a hilly country, the Danites were given an extensive fertile plain leading from the coast towards the hill country. The foothills offered good grazing for their herds, and their land allocation also included woodland suitable for building.

Obviously there was opposition to their settlement and the enemy had the advantage of iron and chariots perfectly suited to the coastal plains. So, despite the assurances of God, we read: "The Amorites confined the Danites to the hill country, not allowing them to come down into the plain" (Judges 1:34). Although their story is found in chapter 18 of Judges, chronologically the narrative fits more into chapters 4 and 5 just prior to the time of the judge Deborah. (This will have significance later, as we shall see.)

The reality of life must have seemed a far cry from the promises they had been given. Where were the milk and honey, the vineyards, and certain prosperity? Being holed up in the foothills and fearful of the occupying Amorites certainly offered the Danites thinking time. Had the long journey over rough terrain and the battles with various enemies really been worth it? Didn't God know what they needed? Hadn't they done enough already? Didn't they deserve an easier time than this? Why couldn't He just slay the Amorites for them?

Discontentment and decision-making

Not prepared to engage in the difficult task of conquering their portion of the land, the Danites decided to look beyond what God had chosen for them and explore their options

117

further afield. Five warriors, in name rather than activity, were sent to explore the land in the hope that they would find somewhere better suited to their "needs". Early on in their journey, these men encountered the Ephraimite Micah and his family. As the Danites were about to discover, we can be sure that when we start looking for solutions outside of God's will, Satan and his demonic followers will take the opportunity to offer a rather attractive alternative. At this time in history, the Israelites were spiritually far away from God as illustrated in Judges 17:6: "In those days Israel had no king; everyone did as he saw fit."

In brief, as an act of thanksgiving to the Lord, Micah and his mother commissioned a silversmith to make an image and an idol, which were then installed in Micah's homemade shrine. Making an ephod (that is, a garment worn by priests during religious ceremonies) out of silver, Micah installed one of his sons to become the family priest, even though they were not from the family of Levi. Soon afterwards it just so happened that a young Levite came to Micah's house looking for work and happily, usurping the son, accepted the offer of becoming the household priest! This is not the book to explore in detail the number of commandments and laws that were broken in just this one story, but it is into this bespoke or personally modified religion that the Danites enter and seek the Lord's "opinion" on their journey north.

Some eighty miles later, the five spies come across the perfect place, Laish, "where they saw that the people were living in safety, like the Sidonians, unsuspecting and secure. And since their land lacked nothing, they were prosperous" (Judges 18:7). It was everything they could have hoped for and all without the need to engage with a powerful enemy. I am reminded of the Scriptures that recount the time when King

Hezekiah and his people, trapped in Jerusalem by the Assyrian army, are offered a false way out of their predicament by the supreme commander.

> Do not listen to Hezekiah. This is what the king of Assyria says: Make peace with me and come out to me. Then each of you will eat fruit from your own vine and fig tree and drink water from your own cistern, until I come and take you to *a land like your own*, a land of grain and new wine, a land of bread and vineyards, a land of olive trees and honey. Choose life and not death! "Do not listen to Hezekiah, for he is misleading you when he says, 'The Lord will deliver us.'"
>
> 2 Kings 18:31–32, emphasis mine

The snowball effect

The five men were so convinced that this was *the* place, that their report back to the people even included a divine endorsement: "When you get there, you will find an unsuspecting people and a spacious land that God has put into your hands, a land that lacks nothing whatever" (Judges 18:10).

Not all of the people chose to leave the land God had given. But, convinced that this land to the north was "of God", 600 armed men along with their wives and children accompanied the five men back to the city of Laish, stopping on the way to pick up their very own priest and the images and the idols that belonged to Micah. This was no ordinary priest that was living contrary to the Levitical code laid down by Moses; this young man was named Jonathan and he was the *actual* grandson of the great man himself (Judges 18:30). Lured by the assurance of a position of importance and influence, Jonathan gladly gathered together the idolatrous objects and

119

joined the relocating group. As predicted, the unsuspecting people of Laish were no match for the armed Danites and were slaughtered mercilessly, their city destroyed by fire.

Everything seemed to have fallen into place. These people, without the dangers of battle, had settled in a good and fertile land far away from Canaanite strongholds. They had a Levite, the grandson of Moses no less, to lead them spiritually, and they also possessed images and idols to help them worship. It all worked out so well, surely God was sanctioning and blessing their decision. Because Shiloh, the ordained place of worship, was some eighty miles away, it seemed reasonable to set up their own altar there in the newly built city, thus saving people the time and trouble of travelling south. And so these people settled down in a land chosen by them, and worshipped in the manner most comfortable and accommodating to their needs.

About 1,200 years later, the apostle Paul writes to his protégé, Timothy: "The sins of some are obvious, reaching the place of judgment ahead of them; the sins of others trail behind them" (1 Timothy 5:24).

What we have in this Danite illustration is a case of "the sins of others trail behind them". So what happened to this renegade band living in the newly built city of Dan? Did their life choices bring a blessing to themselves and others? In not accepting God's gift of land, the tribe travelled north and destroyed a people, a city, and a way of life in order to satisfy their desires. On the way, they rejected God's ordained method of worship and installed a corrupt priest who was happy to adapt accepted protocol in order to meet the needs of his "congregation". This made the community ready to embrace the vision and action of Jeroboam, the first king of Israel, after the division of the land into the northern and southern kingdoms. In a bid to retain his position and hang on to the ten northern tribes, Jeroboam determined to keep the people away from Jerusalem and the southern kingdom of Judah.

> After seeking advice, the king made two golden calves. He said to the people, "It is too much for you to go up to Jerusalem. Here are your gods, O Israel, who brought you up out of Egypt." One he set up in Bethel, and the other in Dan. And this thing became a sin; the people went even as far as Dan to worship the one there.
>
> 1 Kings 12:28–30

Golden calves had led their ancestors astray (Exodus 32) and had the same effect here on God's people. Worshipping a combination of God plus the pagan gods of fertility and strength helped create the area later known as Samaria. This apostasy soon infected large swathes of the Promised Land, ultimately bringing judgment from God. Intermarriage with the Philistines (see the story of Samson in Judges 16) in the allocated land and wilful disobedience from the breakaway tribe in the north ensured its demise. Dan is not listed in the book of 1 Chronicles and, more importantly, it is not listed among the tribes in Revelation 7.

Is God fair?

> Yet no one is immune to the downward spiral of disappointment. It happens to people like the televangelist and to people like the letter writers, and it happens to ordinary Christians: first comes disappointment, then a seed of doubt, then a response of anger or betrayal. We begin to question whether God is trustworthy, whether we can really stake our lives on him.[52]

52 Philip Yancey, *Disappointment with God: Three Questions No One Asks Aloud*, Grand Rapids, MI: Zondervan, 1998, Kindle edition, p. 14.

Next to Judah, Dan was the largest tribe to enter Canaan (Numbers 1:39) and yet not only was it the last to receive its allotment, but it was also given the smallest amount of land. In Deborah's victory song (Judges 5:17), Dan is condemned for not joining in the fighting, but choosing instead to "linger by the ships", implying that the tribe did, at one point, reach the coast before being forced to retreat back to the foothills of the Central Highlands.

Could it be that the Danites had tried, failed, and succumbed to the cycle of thought proposed in the above quote: disappointment, doubt, anger, sense of betrayal? Could it be that a portion of this tribe decided that they were not content with being at the end of the line with only one sweet to enjoy, and chose instead to go and look for what they felt they deserved?

As mentioned at the beginning of the chapter, good parenting requires the mother and father to know their children as individuals and treat them accordingly, determining what is necessary for each son or daughter to thrive. Giving them the right tools and providing the right environment to foster their maturation into adulthood is part of any parent's job description. Most importantly the parents raise their children in an atmosphere of love and security so that the child can trust their parents at all times and in all ways.

I fully appreciate how overwhelming it can be to be told to lay claim to and settle in a land that seems so alien to your natural self. I know a number of men and women who have genuinely tried to make their "land allocation" their home, but have felt worn down by the effort. Are you getting to the end of your endeavours and feel that something has to change?

Between a rock and a hard place

The life of a disciple is full of decision-making. At all times, and in so many different ways, a Christian has to choose between obeying God's directive or following their own thoughts and desires. It is no different for those seeking to bring their gay thoughts, attractions, and longings under Christ's Lordship.

You could commit to a loving, faithful, and monogamous same-sex relationship and worship the Lord, but to do so, you have to be like the Danites – move away from the land God has given you and find a place of compromise. Biblical history shows us that one cannot both fully trust God and still seek one's own solution to the difficulties and challenges that lay ahead. Only God knows fully which people will spend eternity with Him and I certainly have no intention of second-guessing His decision-making. But I do know that the choices we make either enhance or compromise our relationship with the Father. Remember what Jesus said in John 15:10?

> If you obey my commands, you will remain in my love,
> just as I have obeyed my Father's commands and remain
> in his love.

Avoiding our personal Amorites or surrendering to outside pressure will only give a life *like* the one offered by the Lord. But, like wearing a fake Cartier watch or living a life beyond ones financial means, it doesn't matter how many people are misled by the show, you and the Lord know the truth. This is not easy, but we do need to ask ourselves some important questions:

- Are there pockets of compromise in my life?
- How has this compromise impacted my Christian walk?
- Has God's Holy Spirit been unsettling me recently?
- Do I need to reconsider any of the choices I have made?

To stay and flourish in the land the Lord has *chosen for you* requires courage and trust and determined obedience. In the next chapter, Phil and Sonia share with you parts of their long journeys in the Lord.

Section 3

Through the testimonies of Phil and Sonia we see that God gradually modifies our focus from self to Him. Submission and thanksgiving are key components in the life of a disciple and are critical if our same-sex attraction is to come under the Lordship of Christ.

Chapter 7

Questions, Questions, Questions

Around the age of three years, the average child learns one word that can drive an otherwise patient mother to distraction, and that is the monosyllabic word "Why?" As children get older, they create little sentences: *Why are you drinking water? Why are you writing? Why are you cooking?* Sometimes children actually want to know the answer. At other times they simply want to engage with you and experiment in the art of conversation. But around puberty and on into the teenage years the question "Why?" can take on a more defiant, if not sinister, tone and the exploration of social and physical boundaries – along with the sense of responsibility that should accompany encroaching adulthood – is no easy journey for the parent or the child.

Why, God?

There are classic "Why?" questions that are asked in relation to faith, such as, "If God is the God of love, then why does He allow suffering?"; "If God is in control, then why didn't He prevent the tsunami?"; "Why doesn't God make the world love each other?" And then there are the more personal questions like, "Why did my mother die so young?" or "Why can't I conceive?"

At times, when I felt I was getting absolutely nowhere in addressing my same-sex attraction, in frustration I would ask God why I couldn't have a "normal" problem like other people. I'm not sure I had actually compiled a list of "normal" problems, but there were times when I would have willingly traded the seemingly endless bombardment of wrong thoughts for a spot of kleptomania.

There are men and women who say that their attractions toward and temptations to engage in homosexual behaviour have not only completely disappeared, but they have gone on to develop a general attraction towards those of the opposite gender, often resulting in marriage and children. Also, a number of men and women I know have not experienced a great shift in overall same-sex attractions, but God has brought into their lives one particular person of the opposite sex they are able to love, commit to, and delight in a fully satisfying relationship. However our lives pan out, we can be sure that no two stories are the same.

I asked my friends Phil and Sonia to share their stories. Phil is married, Sonia is single. Both have dealt with SSA long term and faithfully, so their narratives offer us some rich lessons in tenacity, perseverance, and grace.

Phil's story

It is impossible to really identify at what point in my life I began to realize that I was attracted to other boys rather than to girls. I am aware that the roots of these attractions go deep into my childhood and I can certainly remember events at around age six or seven that played a part in this. However, it was probably not until I was nineteen and starting university that I realized and began to label what was going on in me as homosexuality.

My first commitment to Jesus was on Easter Sunday 1965. It is the only occasion that I can recall the minister of my church presenting a "gospel message". In this world, I cannot say that anything in my life changed as a result. But conversion is a work of the Spirit and not of man. I think God "marked my card". The badge of my grammar school displayed on my blazer the word "Renascor" – "I have been born again" – a small irony that shows God's sense of humour? It was 19 December 1971, at the end of my first term at university, that I made a recommitment which began to release the transforming power of Christ at work in me. During that term, I realized that I was now free to make decisions for myself about faith and church attendance. I began attending a Methodist church in London with a more evangelical outlook than I was used to and also gathered a group of friends at university from Methodist backgrounds who were seeking God in their lives, especially baptism in the Holy Spirit.

Two questions

I was very challenged by God over two matters at this time: Firstly, was the Bible true? It could either be a book of fairy stories or a book that contained the power of the living God and explains to us who God really is, who we really are, and His relationship to us. If that were the case, none of it can be ignored or dismissed. It is essential for life.

Secondly, did I really acknowledge my sin? After all, I was a good Christian boy, there was nothing particular in my life that I felt I needed to seek God's forgiveness and redemption for – or was there? Well, actually, there was that area of my life that no one knew about – my dark secret: those feelings I had for other boys and that habit of lust and masturbation at least three times a day, not to mention the occasions in my teens when I had crossed boundaries with other boys.

That recommitment in December 1971 was the turning point of acknowledging God's Word was true, whether or not I had an understanding of it or even agreed with it – I had to be enlightened and changed.

I also acknowledged that, despite all my efforts, I was a sinner and only God's grace could give me a right standing with Him.

I am personally convinced that had that encounter with God not occurred, I was most likely to have chosen a path of homosexual promiscuity, and at that time in history, would have contracted HIV and died of AIDS long before now. My university began its Gay Society the next term. Maybe God would have intervened and presented a further opportunity to walk with Him, but there is no guarantee that would have happened.

Those years at university were formative in developing and deepening my life in Christ. In the early 1970s, the Charismatic movement was a major force in British Christianity. Many of us were impacted by Dennis Bennett's books: *Nine O'clock in the Morning* and *The Holy Spirit and You*. Many of us experienced baptism in the Spirit and a few of us spent time visiting a church in a small village in Somerset, South Chard.

Dating and marriage

This church majorly impacted many in the UK during the 1970s, myself and my wife included, and in our case it became instrumental in forming our marriage. Despite my attractions and feelings, my desire in life was for a wife and family. As an only child, I had no sisters to educate me in the ways of girls, or brothers to share how to approach a woman. Jill and I had known each other for about three years as we attended the same church in London. My efforts to ask her to go out with me in February of 1974 had been rebuffed, leaving me disappointed and wondering whether a relationship would ever come my way.

In the August of 1974 I was on holiday in Exeter with

a youth group and decided to make my first visit to South Chard. I hired a car and set off for the Wednesday night meeting where, upon my arrival, I was surprised to find Jill present along with one of her friends. They had taken a detour to the church while travelling to their holiday destination in the Scilly Isles. A few days later, I was even more amazed to discover that Jill had been praying the Sunday before whether she should, after all, go out with me, and that she felt impressed by God to "wait until Wednesday". Our relationship started at that point and we were married one year later in August 1975.

Time for truth

If there was a Hollywood element to this romance, it was much more a romantic comedy. I am not sure that either of us really knew what we'd got ourselves into, but we certainly knew that God had got us into it. At some point, as the relationship became more serious, I felt it was appropriate to share with Jill about my attractions. In doing so, the reason for my being rejected in the February came to light. Jill had been having an affair with an older married man whom we both knew well. Not only that, but in many ways Jill still had a strong romantic attachment to this man.

Humanly speaking, the foundation of our relationship was the sinking sand of my attractions to men and her romantic entanglement with him. But God had taken hold of these two sexually and emotionally broken people and decided we were made for each other; He wanted us together and to give us a testimony that would "bring many from darkness to light". He intended to build this marriage on the rock of Himself: His Word and His ordained covenants.

Submission and reality

Marriage for us was not at all about a romantic whirlwind; it was much more about a submission to a deep sense of God's will. Matthew 6:33 encourages us to seek first the kingdom of God and other things will be added. He has added much to our lives in the last forty years, significantly a deep and long-lasting love for each other, the key foundation of which is His everlasting love for us. He really does give to us all we need for life and godliness (2 Timothy 1:4). He has given us three children and four grandchildren (so far), provided us with an increasing understanding of His Word, financial blessings, ministry, and so much more than we could have expected or anticipated.

So, what happened to all those feelings of attraction to men? I think it would be true to say that for the first twenty-four years of our marriage I lived in denial. They were there and I have to confess that masturbation, fantasy, and sometimes pornography were involved in my continuing secret world. I am, however, deeply grateful that God protected me from becoming involved physically with anyone else other than Jill. Knowing how I felt at times in that period, I do consider that to be a miracle.

A new journey

But eventually, as God works in us and through us, He brings us to the right place and time to deal with our issues on His timetable. For me, that began in August 1999. In preparation for a sermon I was due to preach at my church on return from holiday, God challenged me to allow Him to begin to work on my issues and to start by making myself accountable to a close, trusted friend. That was not easy, and it was four months later before I obeyed. At the time, I think I expected all attractions and feelings for men to disappear within a few months. Once again, however, I discovered that His ways are not our ways and His thoughts not our thoughts. August 1999, like December 1971, became the start of a new journey into the promises of God in this wilderness life.

I began this new leg of my faith journey with another question and asked God, "Why did these feelings develop in me?" It was one of those talks with God where you get an immediate answer: "You don't need to know now!" and I had a picture, which is rare for me, of a tree pulled up exposing its root system (which was a perfectly round ball of tangled stuff). Then I sensed God saying to me, "There is no one thing, but many factors involved that all interlink. Focus now on making good choices, never mind grubbing around in the past, as you can't change it."

Part of this journey has been God's wonderful counsellor, and in His timing the Holy Spirit revealing to me the roots of my attractions over the past few years. I am often asked about how homosexuality is caused and as time goes on, I say less and less about this. I have come to realize that a multitude of factors are involved. Many of those same factors will be present in people who never develop same sex attractions. There is no "if a then b" where homosexuality is concerned. It's more like "if some of a or b or c or d or... then maybe there is x per cent chance of homosexuality". The state of research in this area is way too naive. But God reveals things when it helps us to know them.

For me personally, the main issue amongst many was feeling alienated from other boys as I grew up. There were self-confidence and self-image issues, physical issues, and sometimes simply differences in interests that brought distance from other boys and with distance a degree of envy that became sexualized at puberty. These things and others apply to me and to me alone. If they fit the story of others and help them, so be it. I can't impose my causalities on others. But what God has revealed to me about me has helped me to understand myself more and put into place better ways of controlling my thoughts and actions. That is the important lesson.

Claiming some land

I mentioned that self-confidence was an issue for me, as it is for many. I felt quite alone as a teenager and focused my life on more solitary and intellectual pursuits. This manifested later in having a technically focused job, happier programming computers than relating with people. A very significant transformation took place for me in 1987, when I was selected for some intensive management training as part of my career. God made it very clear that I needed a transformation into a people-person if I were to truly reflect Jesus in my life, because God was essentially people-focused. After all, God is love. While on this management training scheme God began this transformation process. By the end of this course I was no longer working in IT, but managing 170 customer-facing staff and dealing with customer complaints. He had trained me to overcome much of my shyness and lack of self-esteem.

The year 2000 then became another major year for change for me. Not only had a conversation begun with God about my same-sex attraction, but He also brought a change in my work circumstances which led to early retirement at forty-eight and the opening of doors in voluntary work with a number of Christian charities, for which He had trained me in many ways during my secular career.

In 1975, during our period of engagement, Jill and I were given a prophetic word. "You have a testimony. Do not despise your testimony, for through it many will be brought from darkness to light." Some twenty-five years later, in God's perfect timing, my testimony became public knowledge.

Lessons I have learned

There is so much to share from the past fourteen years but I have chosen to highlight some key lessons God has taught me in this journey of facing up to same-sex attraction in my own life:

- *He is much more interested in changing our hearts and in His Spirit empowering us into new behaviours than He is about changing sexual orientation. The Bible never mentions orientation; it focuses on behaviours.*

- *Our identity is not rooted in our sexual attractions, but it is deeply rooted in Him.*

- *Our attractions may not change, but we can be empowered by His Spirit not to engage in sinful behaviours, lust, pornography, etc. – whatever our attractions may be. His forgiveness is readily available for when we fail, but failures become fewer in time.*

- *He does not want us to live in denial, but in light and truth and in self-denial. The challenge is always to take up our cross and follow Him into living a life where some of our desires have to be crucified with Him. The Christian life is not a walk in the park.*

- *Your heart is where you invest it. I have invested my life in my wife, family, church, and ministry.*

- *Nothing is wasted. I could never have known in 1974 that the church in 2014 would be riven by controversy about homosexuality. But God foreknew, and He has been working through my life to help bring His light into the darkness around this issue.*

The over-arching theme of this second journey has been to put into practice what His Word has always been telling me. Painted on the wall in the South Chard church in 1974 were the words, "You shall know the truth and the truth shall set you free." However, the preceding verse – John 8:31 – begins: "If you hold to my teaching then…" Truth and freedom in their reality do not come to us until we begin to obey His teaching. His Lordship of our lives is always the starting point. No longer is freedom a theoretical concept the Bible talks about, but a reality. Why ever did it take me so long to learn?

Does one size fit all?

Phil's story is vastly different from my own and that is why we cannot present a rigid template to those who seek to bring their SSA into line with God's rules. As I understand it there is only one occasion in Christianity when the sentiment behind the phrase "one size fits all" actually rings true, and that is concerning Christ's atoning work on the cross.

This is how much God loved the world: He gave his Son, his one and only Son. And this is why: so that no one need be destroyed; by believing in him, anyone can have a whole and lasting life. God didn't go to all the trouble of sending his Son merely to point an accusing finger, telling the world how bad it was. He came to help, to put the world right again. Anyone who trusts

in him is acquitted; anyone who refuses to trust him
has long since been under the death sentence without
knowing it.

John 3:16–18, *The Message*

As *The Message* version states in verse 17, "Anyone who trusts in
him is acquitted". No one is too small or too large for this gift of
salvation and garment of righteousness. But the outworking of
this salvation is unique to each one and God has commissioned
every individual to complete his or her particular journey both
in Him and with Him.

Sonia is a dear friend whom I first encountered in San
Antonio, Texas, back in 1990. I say "encountered" rather than
"met" because Sonia is quite a dynamic life force and uses to
the full the vast range of gifts and abilities that God has given
her. The following is part of Sonia's story.

Sonia's story

I was raised by two parents who loved me well, who were
very devoted to one another and to me and my older
brother. They delighted in seeing me grow and enjoy
rich pursuits that became a lifeline of joy, from ballet to
chemistry to singing and soldering and welding. Although
human, their example of kindness, integrity, commitment,
and hope for the future continues to be a great strength
and inspiration.

Like many who experience same-sex attraction, I had
the feeling from a young age of being "different" and out
of sync with the larger world of male and female, of men
and women. This caused deep loneliness that was only
partially offset by the love around me, for I intuitively knew
this "difference" would be a heavy burden and would
cause me to have to make difficult choices. By this time,

I had begun to encounter the mysterious and irresistible presence of a much greater Love that called to me from the other side of eternity, which beckoned from the heavens for me to trust and to know He was, and always would be, present.

When my mother encountered Christ about a year later (my father's journey took a bit longer), I first heard His name, and asked Jesus into my heart. I was then three years of age, and this introduction happened just in time because some great trials were ahead. In addition to the burden of feeling different, from the age of seven I suffered multiple instances of sexual molestation from outside of the family that increased the loneliness and put me at great discomfort with my gender.

Throughout my teenage years, I suffered mostly in isolation, though not entirely, as I was able to confide in my mother and know that she was praying for me and that both she and my father loved and believed in me, confident in my future. I did well in school and, though painfully shy and awkward, was reasonably well liked. [School was] where I eagerly explored all areas of learning, particularly the sciences which were, and remain, my first love.

A question of trust

Toward the end of high school I began to be physically and romantically intimate with another high school girl. This lasted for several months until I realized I could not reconcile such a relationship with what I believe God has intended for sexual expression: that it only be between a man and woman. Although I had no basis for knowing whether my feelings would ever change, I concluded that I could trust the One who created me and died for me more than I trusted my own attractional tendencies.

In my twenties, while in college and grad school, I found some measure of rest and joy in the local church, where I was able to work through the sexual abuse and again to feel innocent and confident in relation to both men and women. My friendships were able to deepen and life became full as I entered my chosen profession as a scientist.

Around this time I also pursued healing support in groups focused specifically on serving those with same-sex attractions. Groups such as Desert Stream and inspirational conferences such as those [held] by the late Exodus International connected me with others who were on a journey of trust in the destiny given not by human conceptions of sexual fulfilment, but a vision of love that reflected God's eternal image of male and female.

We are not intended to do this alone. We become by knowing and being known in the lives we touch by being there and the lives through which we are touched. The living stones fit together into a place to belong. The choices we make matter because, whether in identifiable or subtle ways, they make a difference in the lives of others.

The God Almighty whose signature is written in the galaxies, whose pen traces the swirls both of nebula gases and DNA spirals, whose breath is in the expansion of stars and the lifting of tiny leaves in the wind, sees us and lays claim to our lives, inviting us to join Him in His song. This I do and pray others are inspired to do as they recognize His voice calling from beyond eternity.

Why "Why?" isn't the right question

We shall hear more of Sonia's story later, but I am struck by her commitment to "trust and obey", as the old hymn declares, despite attractions and temptations. Similarly to Sonia, I have found that years of obedience to God's Word, submission to accountability groups, periods of fasting and prayer, and addressing particular areas of hurt and trauma through therapy *do not guarantee* the removal of every gay thought or passing attraction. And that is OK. Focusing on *why* some of these misdirected thoughts and feelings linger despite our best efforts to remove them can distract us from what is important to God and to us as His disciples. The Gospel of Matthew[53] tells us that in the Garden of Gethsemane Jesus asked God to take away the cup of suffering and separation that He was about to endure. God heard His Son's entreaty but chose, because of His love for us, not to grant the request. Jesus could have still walked away from the cross but chose, instead, to submit and comply with the Father's wishes.

The apostle Paul suffered from some kind of difficulty or impairment that he would have preferred not to deal with, and asked the Lord three times to remove this "thorn" (2 Corinthians 12:7–8). God assuredly heard Paul's repeated request, but chose not to grant him such immediate release, preferring to give him the option of finding the Father's grace in the midst of the problem. And that is the same option given to every believer today, irrespective of their presenting issue.

Paul learned much from *not* having his prayer answered and I am rather fond of Eugene Peterson's rendition of the Scripture:

> Because of the extravagance of those revelations,
> and so I wouldn't get a big head, I was given the gift
> of a handicap to keep me in constant touch with my
> limitations. Satan's angel did his best to get me down;
> what he in fact did was push me to my knees. No

53   Matthew 26.

danger then of walking around high and mighty! At first I didn't think of it as a gift, and begged God to remove it. Three times I did that, and then he told me,

My grace is enough; it's all you need.
My strength comes into its own in your weakness.

Once I heard that, I was glad to let it happen. I quit focusing on the handicap and began appreciating the gift. It was a case of Christ's strength moving in on my weakness. Now I take limitations in stride, and with good cheer, these limitations that cut me down to size – abuse, accidents, opposition, bad breaks. I just let Christ take over! And so the weaker I get, the stronger I become.

2 Corinthians 12:7–10, *The Message*

I am not, for an instant, suggesting that a person's struggles with SSA are a gift from Satan, and neither would I call it a handicap. But I am encouraging each one of us to adopt Paul's attitude and see these challenges not as a stumbling block to faith, but rather as a springboard into a powerful life in Christ.

I am often asked if I am free from homosexuality, but I think that question begs the bigger question, "What is freedom?" As I mentioned in an earlier chapter, I believe that freedom is not necessarily the lack of desire for something or someone, but it is the absence of compulsion: freedom is the introduction of choice. If we are to dwell in the richness of God's grace and enjoy the freedom He offers, then the first thing we need to do is submit to God's sovereignty. And who better to learn from than Christ and His dear friend and disciple Peter?

Chapter 8

Submission

> We want a certain autonomy, a day off, some out-of-limits, no-go areas.
>
> This unyielded heart will never know and grow in God. The church is full of saved but stunted spiritual pygmies. The person who would have more of God must give more to God. The person who would hear God more must listen more to God. The person who would be filled with the Spirit must relinquish all rights. The Spirit must have free rein through our whole lives, without any compartmentalising or qualifying what he may do or where he may go. Do you desire more of God? Then yield to him. Surrender is the only way to live life in the Spirit.[54]
>
> Simon Ponsonby, *More*

> He withdrew about a stone's throw beyond them, knelt down and prayed, "Father, if you are willing, take this cup from me; yet not my will, but yours be done."
>
> Luke 22:41–42

for one will never be able to comprehend the extent of Christ's humiliation as He knelt among the olive trees and waited for the people He created and loved to drag Him away to a torturous and violent death. In chapter 4, I addressed the need to keep the two commandments that Jesus emphasized in

---

54 Simon Ponsonby, *More: How You Can Have More of the Spirit When You Already Have Everything in Christ*, Victor, 2004, pp. 80, 81.

order: first, to love the Lord your God with all your heart, with all your soul, with your entire mind; and second, to love your neighbour as yourself (see Matthew 22:37–39). I wrote about creating a framework of truth and seeking to live out of that framework not only by fostering a more intimate relationship with the Father, but also by using it as a means of protection as we reach out horizontally to the various "neighbours" who cross our path.

The need for humility

> Once you were alienated from God and were enemies in your minds because of [as shown by] your evil behaviour.

Colossians 1:21

My natural mind is totally contrary to the things of God and, more often than not, I want to do things my way and in my own time. Today's Western society applauds the individuals who know what they want and will fight for their right to have those needs and wants met. The only proviso society stipulates is that *no one gets hurt in the process* and that, of course, is one of those well-meaning but ultimately useless stipulations that can't possibly be upheld. For example, a divorce, no matter how amicable, signifies the breakdown of a love and commitment that once filled two people with hope and joy, and cannot possibly be agreed to without pain and a sense of loss over what has gone. And if there are children resulting from the marriage, then the hurt is magnified and multiplied a number of times over. In a society that does its level best to avoid having to feel hurt, pain, or discomfort of any kind, we are remarkably adroit at inflicting it, wittingly or unwittingly, on those around us.

Jesus could only fulfil His commission by standing in and operating out of an unbroken relationship with God. On earth, despite being tempted in all things (Hebrews 4:15), He managed to remain in that vertical framework of total surrender. Undoubtedly Jesus had demands from the horizontal plane of relationships, but no love – not even for His mother and family – usurped His love for His Father. No reasoning, no matter how profound, could shake His faith in the One Jesus stood with at the creation of the world, and no commitment to His own race overrode His primary obligation to complete His work on earth and bring salvation to all. We are triune beings made in the image of God and our spirit, soul, and body need to be ensconced within the security of the vertical if we are to minimize our proclivity to sin. And this is, quite frankly, a vexation to our soul. While God tells us that true freedom is found in submission and surrender to His ways, our natural self is not wired for a renunciation of all that we hold to be rightfully ours or full compliance to the will of another. It is primed for independent self-determination. We believe ourselves to be masters of our own universe and any expression of acquiescence is seen as a sign of weakness.

> Do not love the world or anything in the world. If anyone loves the world, the love of the Father is not in him. For everything in the world – the cravings of sinful man, the lust of his eyes and the boasting of what he has and does – comes not from the Father but from the world. The world and its desires pass away, but the man who does the will of God lives forever.
>
> 1 John 2:15–17

How hard it is to live as a sign of contradiction in our thoughts, words, and deeds. In his book *Absolute Surrender* Andrew Murray writes:

> The cause of the weakness of your Christian life is that you want to work it out partly, and to let God help you. And that cannot be. You must come to be utterly helpless, to let God work, and God will work gloriously. It is this that we need if we are indeed to be workers for God.[55]

J. B. Phillips, in his translation of the well-known passage from Philippians 2, writes: "but [Jesus] stripped himself of all privilege by consenting to be a slave by nature" (verse 6). It was in that place of humility that He was able to be an empty vessel ready for God to have all of His fullness dwell in Him (Colossians 1:19). As Christ so perfectly demonstrated while living on this earth, true humility has nothing to do with how badly I think of myself, but arises from being filled with the fullness of God and that includes His wisdom. The greater my understanding of who I am in relation to God the Father and my ability to live out of that truth on a daily basis determines the success, or otherwise, of bringing my natural self and all of its waywardness under the Lordship of Christ.

To live experientially in the truth that I am a co-heir with Jesus (Galatians 4:7), and that I am seated in the heavenlies with Him (Ephesians 2:6), and confident that I have been given every spiritual blessing in Christ (Ephesians 1:3) – that is what enables me to explore and engage in life along the horizontal plane, equipped with sufficient power to say "no" to the trap of emotional dependency, or the lure of gay pornography, or the momentary release of a sexual encounter. It means that I can

55 Andrew Murray, *Absolute Surrender*, optimized for Kindle, p. 54.

participate, with increased confidence, in a life in community finally free from that once ever-present, gnawing emptiness that silently demanded to be filled. The more I live out of that fullness found in my vertical relationship with God, the easier I will find it to serve rather than snatch, to love rather than lust, and to be a blessing rather than a burden to my brothers and sisters in Christ.

Although we know little about Christ's early years, we read in Luke 2 that Jesus was inadvertently left in Jerusalem one Passover while His parents set off home. Losing the impending Messiah and hope for the whole world produced, unsurprisingly, a panicked response from both Mary and Joseph. Their hurried return to Jerusalem found Him, eventually, in the Temple courts learning from and talking with the teachers. Luke calmly concludes the eventful story with: "And Jesus grew in wisdom and stature, and in favour with God and men" (verse 52).

Fostering and developing the understanding that He was *fully* reliant on God allowed the Father not only to dwell in Him, but also to be made manifest in Him. This was evident particularly throughout His three years of ministry that culminated in the ultimate submission: that of giving His life for the salvation of all who believe in Him. Christ's final submission to death *unleashed* God's victorious power into His world.

Peter's rocky road of discipleship

Peter had no problem in making a full-blown decision to be with Jesus and readily left his career in fishing. It took just one word from Jesus and we read in Matthew 4 that both Peter and his brother Andrew *immediately* left their nets and followed Him. Peter's faith in his Lord continued at a pace. And, while the rest of the disciples were crying out in fear,

Peter alone took Jesus at His word, quite literally at one word, "Come," and stepped out of the boat (Matthew 14:22–32). Peter also had spiritual insight and when Jesus asked, "Who do you think I am?" Simon Peter was quick to answer, "You are the Messiah, the Son of the living God" (Matthew 16:16). After having witnessed countless miracles and listened to awe-inspiring teaching for three consecutive years, Peter was a fully paid up Christ-follower.

> But after I am raised [to life], I will go before you into Galilee. But Peter said to Him, Even if they all fall away and are caused to stumble and distrust and desert You, yet I will not [do so]!And Jesus said to him, Truly I tell you, this very night, before a cock crows twice, you will utterly deny Me [disclaiming all connection with Me] three times. But [Peter] said more vehemently and repeatedly, [Even] if it should be necessary for me to die with You, I will not deny or disown You! And they all kept saying the same thing.
>
> Mark 14:28–31, AMP

So confident was Peter in his love for Jesus that he could declare boldly his readiness to die with and for his friend. After all, hadn't Peter walked away from his career, lived without the security of a regular income, relied on others to provide him with food and shelter, and created enemies by following this Jesus? Of course Peter wasn't going to turn back now when he had come this far. When given the chance earlier, Peter had been quite adamant as to where his commitment lay:

"You do not want to leave too, do you?" Jesus asked the Twelve.Simon Peter answered him, "Lord, to whom shall we go? You have the words of eternal life. We have come to believe and to know that you are the Holy One of God."

John 6:67–69

The reason why so many of us love Peter is that we hear our own voice in his declarations of faith. Like him, we sacrificially give up much of our life in response to the Lord's leading, and we33 too, like dear Peter, often fail to deliver when the rubber hits the road. How often have I wept bitterly when my Christian walk has not lived up to my Christian talk? How often are you disappointed with the outworking of your faith?

An illustration from marriage

When a couple decide to marry and publicly declare their love for one another in a marriage ceremony, no one present is expecting them to immediately think and behave as a mature married couple. And the same is true of someone who has made a decision to follow Jesus: it is OK to be an immature Christian *if that is what you are*. But problems arise when a believer fails to mature in their faith. One would expect a couple celebrating their golden wedding anniversary to have developed in their relationship during those fifty years of marriage. Grand, even ostentatious overtures of love will have mellowed into a gentle "knowing" of and devotion to the partner.

Similarly, saying the sinner's prayer and making a commitment to Jesus is not the same as making a decision to *follow* Jesus. Both commitment in marriage and commitment to follow Jesus is the capacity *to carry out* the decision the person has made, even if the initial heady emotions have somewhat faded.

I remember Dennis Nolan, a former pastor of mine, saying, "Any fool can get married, but it takes special people to keep a marriage going." May I venture to say that for people given to same-sex attraction, a decision to follow Christ requires that same constrained dedication?

From failure to failure

What can we learn from Peter? How did he progress from his impetuous immature faith in Jesus into someone the apostle Paul later described as a "pillar" of the church (Galatians 2:9)? Failure, real or perceived, in any walk of life can prompt us to return to old ways of living. For some of us, that has meant re-running old sinful tapes around in our thought life, or returning to past relationships or behaviours in an effort to seek solace. For Peter, having denied and abandoned Jesus, his failure meant going back to work and fending for himself.

What is interesting is that, despite having met with the resurrected Christ on at least two occasions, Peter *still* determined to do his own thing and took off to the shore of the lake. It shouldn't escape our notice either that, even though he was not yet a leader, his decision influenced seven other disciples who followed his example and returned to their former occupation. Not surprisingly this self-determined course of action brought no success and the night's labour proved fruitless; Peter had failed as a disciple and now he had failed as a fisherman.

From failure to faith

And when the disciples have exhausted themselves in fruitless toil throughout the night, always indicative of spiritual darkness, Jesus Himself intervenes. And Christ's provision is in stark contrast to their self-made plight. At His word the nets are filled, because of His thoughtfulness there is fire to warm their tired bodies, and from His own hands there is food prepared to fill their hungry bellies. Most importantly, of course, is that this meeting on the shore of Galilee as a group gives opportunity for Jesus to meet and speak with Peter as an individual. Scholars differ on the length of time that had transpired between Christ's resurrection and His intimate talk with Peter, but there is agreement that it would have been at least ten days between these two events.

What a long time since Peter had heard that cock crow, proving the truth of Christ's warning that Peter's faith would fail under pressure. Understandably then, Peter sits on the shore that morning as a broken man devoid of any confidence in himself and it is there, at that point of abject weakness, that Jesus not only restores the relationship but He also gives Peter a ministry and then commissions him into service.

> When they had finished breakfast Jesus said to Simon Peter, "Simon, son of John, do you love me more than these others?" "Yes, Lord," he replied, "you know that I am your friend." "Then feed my lambs," returned Jesus. Then he said for the second time, "Simon, son of John, do you love me?" "Yes, Lord," returned Peter. "You know that I am your friend." "Then care for my sheep," replied Jesus. Then for the third time, Jesus spoke to him and said, "Simon, son of John, are you my friend?" Peter was deeply hurt because Jesus' third question to him was "Are you my friend?", and he said, "Lord, you know everything. You know that I am your friend!"
>
> John 21:15–17, J. B. PHILLIPS

Peter was a man who had followed Jesus wholeheartedly up until that fateful evening in the courtyard of the high priest. He had willingly abandoned his career and given up a regular income and a straightforward home life in response to Christ's call. Peter had done all that he could to be a disciple worthy of his Lord. And it had resulted in dismal failure. For what must have seemed like perpetuity, Peter had lived with the knowledge that his best was not good enough and now, at this point on the shore of Lake Galilee, Jesus was asking him to give up the one thing that prevented him from becoming truly godly.

So now, asks Jesus, in the light of recent events, *Peter, do you love Me more than these other men love Me? Do you love Me above all other things? Peter, do you even love Me as a friend?*

The old Peter would have jumped in like some soppy Labrador, confident of his love for his master and confident of his master's love for him. But events had changed Peter. He no longer had confidence in himself to live a life of faith, and now knew that he was only ever one breath away from denying his Lord. When asked by Jesus the depth of love that he carried for his friend, Peter trusts solely in Jesus' opinion: "Lord, *you* know everything. *You* know that I am your friend!" (emphasis mine). For all of his commitment and service, Peter was always limited by his own enthusiastic drive. But now, emptied of self, Peter was at last ready to walk in the footsteps of Jesus. Andrew Murray writes:

> We must learn of Jesus, how He is meek and lowly of heart. He teaches us where true humility takes its rise and finds its strength – in the knowledge that it is God who worketh all in all, that our place is to yield to Him in perfect resignation and dependence, in full consent to be and do nothing of ourselves.[56]

56   Andrew Murray, *Humility: The Beauty of Holiness* (Ichthus Publications, 2014) Kindle edition, p. 19.

We worship an awesome God and when we have failed and turned back to Him in confession and repentance, our heavenly Father is eager to meet with us again. When God restores each one of us into a relationship with Him, He is not like a human leader or boss who sends us back to square one to teach us a lesson. Jesus didn't say to Peter, "Well, I'm glad you've declared your love for Me, but you've blown it as a disciple. Go back to your fishing and be content to 'follow Me from afar' just like you did the night before I died." No, Jesus not only restored Peter to fellowship with Him, but gave him *greater responsibility* in His kingdom. Stripped of confidence in his own ability to follow and serve, Peter was now in the perfect place of service because his confidence was fully transferred into Christ's ability to keep and lead him.

We all fall short

I fear that many Christians echo Peter's life up until this point of restoration and responsibility. They begin their Christian walk as keen new believers, eager to learn all there is to know about Jesus and this new life of faith. In the early days, all hardships and deprivation seem a small price to pay for the new life they have found in their Saviour.

And it is often during this period that those who see homosexual behaviour as incongruent with their Christian faith first pursue help, often spurred on by a hope or even expectation of attractional change. Keen to apply God's truth to somewhat disordered or dysfunctional parts of our life, we actively seek Him, get professional therapy, and/or attend ministries and read books that offer help. But even if we do not engage in sinful behaviour, at some point there will be a hiatus in this journey, and, at some point, like Peter, our best efforts will fail.

Despite having found much help and hope at Desert Stream Ministries and various conferences, and because of her application to personal growth, my friend Sonia still experienced a crossroads in her life. She writes:

> At the same time I was faced with a dilemma in that some twenty years after starting on this journey, I saw no discernible signs of attraction to the opposite sex, even after the most in-depth and transparent reckoning of any feature of my past or personal background that might be a blockage. I began to wonder if I had failed, or more fundamentally if I had not understood what was being asked of me. Many in my circle of friends were beginning to embrace a pro-gay interpretation of Scripture in relation to sexuality and I knew that I needed to follow my heart in asking questions that might lead into unexpected territory.

In 1999 I faced a similar quandary. Despite fifteen years of applied Christianity, I could not say, hand on heart, that my feelings of same-sex attraction had disappeared. I was a changed woman, for sure, but then I would expect to be different given the fact that I now sought to follow a life based on biblical truth rather than a fallible society. My fundamental way of thinking was far removed from what it once was, but I also knew that it would not take too much encouragement or too many wrong choices for my same-sex thoughts, feelings, and desires to resurface. Like Sonia, I knew of a number of men and women who had also failed to travel along this alleged continuum towards heterosexuality and had chosen instead to return to their proverbial fishing boats. For the most part, these friends had not given up on God, but had lost faith in the apparent promise of change or, at least, in their own ability to enact such change.

What does God actually want?

God doesn't want a mixture of His planning and power mixed with our best efforts. However it happens, I venture to say that we are all given an opportunity to meet with Jesus on, as it were, the shores of Lake Galilee. Part of our growth is to come to the realization that a powerful Christian walk is *not* Jesus plus me, but is Jesus in me. Jesus told His disciples:

> Come to me, all of you who are weary and over-burdened, and I will give you rest! Put on my yoke and learn from me. For I am gentle and humble in heart and you will find rest for your souls. For my yoke is easy and my burden is light.
>
> Matthew 11:28–30, J. B. PHILLIPS

To be gentle and humble in heart comes only from the divine because our natural self is filled with the pride that says, "I choose to live life according to my rules and my desires." Peter had to come to the end of self before he could open the door for God's presence to dwell in and be made manifest through him. And we, too, need to come to the end of our self-effort, no matter how noble, and find true rest for our souls.

Lifting up

In John 15:2 we read that God, the gardener, "lifts" (Greek: airó) off the floor the branch that bears no fruit so it is better exposed to light and air. Peter had already been judge and jury over his own behaviour, and had condemned himself to the job he had before Jesus ever arrived on the scene: he returned to fishing. Having assigned his Christ-following walk to the annals of history, convinced that even if there was a way back into fellowship, there certainly was no way back into service, Peter had condemned himself to a life sentence of mediocrity. Who knows, over time he may even have been able to dismiss those three exciting years with Jesus as a mere emotional blip in his youthful life.

And yet Jesus came to the shoreline and made preparations to welcome and restore Peter. It is always God's intention to lift and restore the branch that has fallen, and to ensure that it not only stays connected to the vine but is also placed in a favourable position that is open to light, warmth, and air. Are you or do you know of anyone who needs the care and attention offered by our Lord today? Sonia had not embarked on a journey of self-determination, but she, much like me, had to experience Christ in a new deeper way. She writes:

> And so I began a period of reflection, of questioning, of weighing the different schools of thought and, most importantly, listening for the voice of my True Love as He led me to take this step of deeper faith. In that time, I encountered yet deeper currents of His love, in a territory that grew larger, more wild, and more joyous. Out of that time of listening it became clear that I had not heard amiss, but that I was exactly where He had wanted me to be. I had not misunderstood that same-sex relations were not my destiny, but I had taken on human criteria of success as measured by whether there was a shift of attractions. This was not an expectation He had imposed. All He had ever wanted was for me to love Him, to go to deep places of the heart with total openness of being, transformed and becoming increasingly the woman He envisioned from before the beginning of time, growing into someone who could abide, who could embody His grace and patience and peace, who could live each moment to glorify the One who had given Himself for mankind.
>
> For the first time, I was truly free. The burden that had weighed so heavily upon me from the time I was a

child lifted, and I experienced a joy and lightness of being I had never known. Although some in my circle of treasured others walking their respective journeys could not accept that I could be at peace with an ongoing attractional tendency and therefore dismissed me, it did not matter. My limbs were unbound and I could run forward with much greater confidence and exuberance, and I have never looked back.

Taking Jesus at His word

Throughout his three years of being a follower of Christ, Peter took Jesus at His word and responded accordingly. While often resulting in personal embarrassment and the occasional good soaking, this characteristic held him in good stead for his restoration into fellowship and service. We never read about Peter refusing to serve because "he once denied his Lord" or that he laboured under the guilt of his past offences. Peter took Jesus at His word and moved on. I am reminded of three Scriptures in Isaiah:

"Forget the former things; do not dwell on the past.
See, I am doing a new thing!"

Isaiah 43:18–19

"I, even I, am he who blots out your transgressions, for my own sake, and remembers your sins no more."

Isaiah 43:25

"I have swept away your offences like a cloud, your sins like the morning mist. Return to me, for I have redeemed you."

Isaiah 44:22

155

Fortunately, God's ability to forgive and restore is far greater than our ability to sin.

Peter needed more

There were ten days between Christ's ascension into heaven and the feast of Pentecost, or Feast of Weeks, and in that time Peter had assumed the role of leader and had overseen the appointment of the new disciple, Matthias. But the arrival of God's Holy Spirit transformed the apostles' lives forever and it was Peter who was given the responsibility to proclaim the first gospel message. Remember that this was the man who only weeks earlier had denied Jesus in the dark courtyard and now here he was, openly proclaiming Him in broad daylight. This was the man who had been fearful of one powerless female servant but now had the confidence to speak before both Roman and Jewish authorities.

On that Pentecost morning Peter stood before the crowds in Jerusalem and eloquently spoke of Jesus as the Messiah. In Acts 2:41 we read: "Those who accepted his message were baptized, and about three thousand were added to their number that day." Not a bad response for someone's first ever sermon!

Transformation is a continual process

I talked about land allocation back in chapter 6 and I must ask: are you experiencing difficulty settling in your "land allocation"? Were you expecting something different, something much easier than the "lot" you've received? Have you been working hard at your transformation and are now feeling too weary to continue? Are you disheartened by your progress or discouraged when others seemingly give up and return to homosexual behaviour? Are you sure you are focusing on the right goal?

Peter's transformation was a continual business of bringing him into conformity to the likeness of Christ and seeing this life from God's viewpoint. Amazingly, God entrusted Peter with the responsibility of declaring mind-blowing truth to Jew and Gentile alike, and he was often a holy conduit through which God performed miracles, signs, and wonders. But, and I find this reassuring, Peter still made mistakes and he was famously confronted publicly by the apostle Paul for reverting back to the Jewish custom of eating separately from the Gentiles (Galatians 2). In his humiliation, the old Peter may well have thrown up his hands in failure and stomped off back to the fishing boats. But this new and altogether more submissive Peter accepted the public rebuke and pressed on to fulfil God's purposes for his life despite his leadership position. In truth, what often differentiates one Christian from another is not the number of sins we commit or mistakes that we make but what we do after the deed has happened. The apostle Paul later wrote,

Do not conform any longer to the pattern of this world, but be transformed by the renewing of your mind. Then you will be able to test and approve what God's will is – his good, pleasing and perfect will.

Romans 12:2

Peter had to live out that truth long before it was ever written down for us to follow suit. He had to lay down a lifetime of human understanding in order to take up God's perception of how life ought to be. Peter grasped hold of this second chance and ran with it. Thus he was transformed from a fisherman to a follower of Christ, from a follower of Christ to a friend of Jesus, and from a friend of Jesus to the father of the church. Peter is the man who is able to write about suffering and trials as follows:

157

> I know how great this makes you feel, even though
> you have to put up with every kind of aggravation in
> the meantime. Pure gold put in the fire comes out of
> it *proved* pure; genuine faith put through this suffering
> comes out *proved* genuine. When Jesus wraps this all
> up, it's your faith, not your gold that God will have on
> display as evidence of his victory.
>
> 1 Peter 1:6–7, *The Message*, my emphasis

Peter's own testimony can be summed up in 1 Peter 5:10–11 (emphasis mine):

> And the God of all grace, who called you to his eternal
> glory in Christ, after you have suffered a little while,
> *will himself restore you and make you strong, firm and
> steadfast*. To him be the power for ever and ever. Amen.

Peter didn't dwell on his failures, but used what he had learned to lead and equip others.

For the purposes of this book, I have called upon men and women who have known the Lord for over twenty years and have addressed or are still addressing their struggles with unwanted same-sex attraction and/or gender identity. Some have given permission to use part or all of their testimony, while others have kindly read an early draft of the book and offered their invaluable thoughts and suggestions to improve the content and text. All of them hold, or have held, leadership positions in Christian ministry, and all of them along the way have made questionable, unhelpful, or even downright wrong decisions at some point in their Christian journey. What sets them apart from other men and women who also began journeying away from a homosexual outlook, attitude, identity, or behaviour is that they humbled and submitted themselves to the One who is able to give a second chance.

Have you, like Peter, been your own judge and jury and condemned yourself to mediocrity because you have been inconsistent in your Christian walk? Have you disqualified yourself from Christian service because you still contend with inner struggles? Have you returned to your personal "fishing boat", convinced that there is no way back for you? Are you tired of fishing and the poor returns? Maybe, like Sonia and me, you haven't actually walked away into sinful behaviour, but certainly need a fresh encounter with Jesus.

Jesus is on the shore with a fire lit to warm you and fine food to fill you up. Most importantly, He is there, longing to sit with you and fully restore your friendship with Him.

The last word goes to Sonia:

> What does the future hold? Often He does not reveal it to us as humans, and I am no exception. Whether I continue as I am or am surprised (as many have been) by falling in love with someone of the opposite sex, life is full and I am content. Although I experience attractions towards women, I identify it only as a tendency and something I experience, not the essential feature of who I am – namely a woman who abides in the love of God. Though a tendency that I do not act upon sexually, it has afforded me much as a vehicle through which I have drawn close to Christ. I trust how He works and I trust Him with my future.

Chapter 9

Thanksgiving is a Weapon of Warfare

> When you have eaten and are satisfied, praise the
> Lord your God for the good land he has given
> you. Be careful that you do not forget the Lord
> your God, failing to observe his commands, his
> laws and his decrees that I am giving you this day.
> Otherwise, when you eat and are satisfied, when
> you build fine houses and settle down, and when
> your herds and flocks grow large and your silver
> and gold increase and all you have is multiplied,
> then your heart will become proud and you will
> forget the Lord your God, who brought you out of
> Egypt, out of the land of slavery.
>
> Deuteronomy 8:10–14

Moses had led these truculent people through the wilderness for forty years and now, even though he personally was barred from entering the Promised Land, this man of God prepared his people to take hold of their inheritance. He warned them of the dangers of forgetting their history and the God who had rescued, provided for, and sustained them during these years. Do what the Lord has commanded, says Moses, and all will go well with you, but start thinking and acting independently from the ways of God and it will all end in failure.

I am sure that this seemed reasonable (at the time) to the twelve tribes as they stood waiting to inherit God's blessings. After forty hot and tiring years, the thought of making a home and staying in one place must have created a palpable sense of expectation within their ranks and a mob-induced belief that the hard part was well and truly behind them. It is easy to give God thanks and praise when all is well and when He lives up to our expectations of how He is to act toward us and for us; the challenge, however, is to give thanks at all times and in all circumstances (1 Thessalonians 5:18).

Foundational faith

The biblical order to dwell in God's presence is known by many and is laid out succinctly in Psalm 100:4: "Enter his gates with thanksgiving and his courts with praise; give thanks to him and praise his name." There is, however, a precursor to thanksgiving and it is stated in the first half of verse 5: "For the Lord is good and his love endures for ever." Do you *know and believe* that the Lord is good? If I am to choose to stand in this framework of truth – loving the Lord with my whole heart, mind, and strength, irrespective of how I feel and however tempting some features of same-sex relationships may seem – I need to know that God is good. If that truth is not residing in the depth of my being, then I will be unable to praise Him in all circumstances and will open myself up to the fiery darts of Satan.

In the Garden of Eden, the devil sowed a seed of doubt in Eve's mind about the goodness of God. That led her to question God's attitude and actions toward her. Having offered up the first question, "Did God say?", Satan then planted the seed:

> The serpent told the Woman, "You won't die. God knows that the moment you eat from that tree, you'll see what's really going on. You'll be just like God, knowing everything, ranging all the way from good to evil."
>
> **Genesis 3:4–5, *The Message***

In forbidding you to eat of this fruit, implies Satan, God is withholding something from you so that He remains all-powerful. If God were good, He would share everything with you. If God were *really* good and He *really* loved you, He would allow you to eat from whatever tree you wanted. If God denies you the fruit of this tree, whispers the devil, then what else is He not letting you have? Eve accepted Satan's reasoning, and we know that she went ahead and ate some of the forbidden fruit, putting into motion the consequences of disobedience that remain with us today.

Doubt is the door to disobedience

Once I accept an element of doubt over God's innate goodness, I've opened the door to disobedience and sin. If I do not believe that God is fully and completely good, then I will be left wondering at what point and in what given situation God is *not* good. If my perspective of God changes from seeing Him as 100 per cent good to 98 per cent good, then I am left with the 2 per cent doubt that will dictate my thought life and influence my behaviour. Any time I doubt His goodness, I can give myself permission to disobey His commands. It goes without saying that I will most question His goodness when I find that He puts boundaries around or prohibits behaviours in which my flesh wants to engage.

We live with the consequences of Adam and Eve's disobedience to God's one prohibition in that glorious garden. Did God tell them not to eat of the fruit in order to spoil their fun? Or was it an expression of His goodness and protection towards them? God said no to the fruit because He knew that if they ate it, they would have knowledge of evil and it was that first-hand knowledge, once the fruit had been tasted, that immediately produced feelings of fear and shame and separation from God. One could reasonably argue that Eve did not understand why God forbade them to eat of this tree, but her belief in the goodness of God should have been enough to know that a good God makes good rules.

The same is true for all of us: if I am fully convinced of the foundational goodness of God, then I will accept, even if I don't fully understand, that God's prohibition on same-gender sexual behaviour is good and emanates from a place of love. In Genesis 1:31 we read: "God looked over everything he had made; it was so good, so very good!" (*The Message*). Just as it requires a pear tree to produce pears, God must be extremely good if He is to create something that is "so very good".

If we are to bring our lives under the Lordship of Christ, then it is critical that we know, without a shadow of a doubt, that God is good and the struggles we may have to endure come because God is for us and not against us and, above all, loves us with an everlasting love.

A brief history of "God is good"

The verbal acknowledgment that God is good appears to be first sung by King David after the ark of the covenant is brought back to Jerusalem (1 Chronicles 16:34) and is then adopted by the designated worshippers who ministered before the Lord. The phrase was certainly declared when the Temple was completed and dedicated during Solomon's reign:

> The trumpeters and singers joined in unison, as with one voice, to give praise and thanks to the Lord. Accompanied by trumpets, cymbals and other instruments, they raised their voices in praise to the Lord and sang: "He is good; his love endures for ever." Then the temple of the Lord was filled with a cloud, and the priests could not perform

> their service because of the cloud, for the glory of the
> Lord filled the temple of God.
>
> **2 Chronicles 5:13–14**

We read that after Solomon had prayed:

> When all the Israelites saw the fire coming down and
> the glory of the Lord above the temple, they knelt on
> the pavement with their faces to the ground, and they
> worshipped and gave thanks to the Lord, saying, "He is
> good; his love endures for ever."
>
> **2 Chronicles 7:3**

Some 450 years later, when the returning exiles lay the foundation stone of the Second Temple, we hear a similar cry from all the people: "He is good; his love to Israel endures for ever" (Ezra 3:11). As if that wasn't enough, Psalms 106 and 107 begin, and Psalm 118 opens and closes with the now familiar phrase: "he is good; his loves endures for ever." And if we hadn't quite got the message, the responsorial Psalm 136 rather drives home the message that God's "love endures for ever"!

The "Passover Hymn" is considered to be contained within Psalm 115 through to Psalm 118; this would have been the hymn sung by Jesus and His disciples that Mark mentions in 14:26, just prior to Christ's time in the Garden of Gethsemane. The final verse of Psalm 118 is: "Give thanks to the Lord, for he is good; his love endures for ever." With those words still on His lips, Jesus walked to the Garden of Gethsemane, thus beginning the final countdown towards His ultimate test. We can be sure that Jesus was not thanking God for the physical pain He was about to endure, nor was it for the fact that His mother would have to watch Him die in agony. It certainly wasn't for the truth that He who knew no sin was about to become sin and experience separation from the Father. There was only one reason that this fully human Jesus could possibly be thanking God: He was *convinced* that God is good and that God is Love.

Love is shown through character

Jesus was able to face those terrible days in Jerusalem because He *knew the character of God* and the great news is that that knowledge is also available to each one of us. It doesn't mean that we won't experience loss, pain, or suffering – because we will. But it does mean that during those times when God may seem distant or silent or uninvolved, we can trust and rely on His character.

In knowing God's true character, we can remain in a position of thanksgiving, irrespective of our situation. And that is a very strong place in which to stand. Only the unswerving belief in the goodness and love of God could have sustained Jesus during that violent, terrifying, and excruciatingly painful time and the great news is that, through His Holy Spirit, we too are able to stand reliant on the goodness of God.

Thanksgiving requires humility

We return now to the importance of humility that we first looked at in chapter 8.

> For this is what the high and exalted One says – he who lives forever, whose name is holy: "I live in a high and holy place, but also with the one who is contrite and lowly in spirit, to revive the spirit of the lowly and to revive the heart of the contrite."
>
> **Isaiah 57:15**

The apostle Paul pulls no punches when he asks the Corinthians, "What do you have that the Lord hasn't given you?" (1 Corinthians 4:7, NLT). Essentially Paul is asking the believers, "Who makes you different from anyone else? What do you have that you did not receive? And if you did receive it, why do you boast as though you did not?"

Are those questions not relevant to every believer? What does any one of us have that the Lord has not given us, for surely we are dependent on Him to provide us with the very next breath?

In Job 41:11 God questions the men: "Who has a claim against me that I must pay? Everything under heaven belongs to me." Paul echoes God's statement in Romans 11:34–35: "Who has known the mind of the Lord? Or who has been his counsellor? Who has ever given to God, that God should repay them?"

And there is the crux of the matter: "Who has ever given to God, that God should repay them?"

Thanksgiving is a choice

Thanksgiving is not an automatic response to the goodness of God. In the Western world, we recognize that the majority of people tend to ignore God until something bad happens, and then they blame and get angry at Him. The first chapter of Romans is often the first "go-to" Scripture when someone wants to preach against homosexual behaviour, and one cannot deny that the subject is certainly mentioned. However, there is so much more to this Scripture that has relevance for all people and not just for the chosen few. Let us remind ourselves of what is said in the New Living Translation.

But God shows his anger from heaven against all sinful, wicked people who suppress the truth by their wickedness. They know the truth about God because he has made it obvious to them. For ever since the world was created, people have seen the earth and sky. Through everything God made, they can clearly see his invisible qualities – his eternal power and divine nature. So they have no excuse for not knowing God.

Yes, they knew God, but they wouldn't worship him as God or even give him thanks. And they began to think up foolish ideas of what God was like. As a result, their minds became dark and confused. Claiming to be wise, they instead became utter fools. And instead of worshiping the glorious, ever-living God, they worshiped idols made to look like mere people and birds and animals and reptiles.

So God abandoned them to do whatever shameful things their hearts desired. As a result, they did vile and degrading things with each other's bodies. They traded the truth about God for a lie. So they worshiped and served the things God created instead of the Creator himself, who is worthy of eternal praise! Amen. That is why God abandoned them to their shameful desires. Even the women turned against the natural way to have sex and instead indulged in sex with each other. And the men, instead of having normal sexual relations with women, burned with lust for each other. Men did shameful things with other men, and as a result of this sin, they suffered within themselves the penalty they deserved. Since they thought it foolish to acknowledge God, he abandoned them to their foolish thinking and let them do things that should never be done. Their lives became full of every kind of wickedness, sin, greed, hate, envy, murder, quarrelling, deception, malicious behaviour, and gossip. They are backstabbers, haters of God, insolent, proud, and boastful. They invent new ways of sinning, and they disobey their parents. They refuse to understand, break their promises, are heartless, and have no mercy. They know God's justice requires that those who do these things deserve to die, yet they do them anyway. Worse yet, they encourage others to do them, too.

Romans 1:18–32, NLT

Paul's argument is succinct:

- I only have to look around to know the truth that God is the Creator
- I see His power to create
- I see His character in the variety, quality, and abundance of all that I see.

Therefore:

- I acknowledge Him as God
- I acknowledge Him for what He does
- I thank Him accordingly.

The downward spiral

At this point, however, the apostle points out the serious consequences in not following this basic pattern. From verse 21, I learn that choosing not to acknowledge the truth of God and what He does means I shut myself off from all connection with the Spirit of Truth. Having rejected divine Truth I automatically limit my capacity to discern what is right. This refusal to be open to the divine inevitably restricts me to the finite thinking of self and society. Consequently, if I choose not to walk in the light of Truth, then I am immediately subjected to walking in darkness and open myself up to all kinds of other voices and influences.

If I continue not to acknowledge His sovereignty in all matters and remain closed to the Spirit of Truth, I am left only with the thoughts of man. Unfortunately the downward spiral does not end there. Verse 22 states: "Claiming to be wise, they instead became utter fools." My self-declaration of wisdom automatically rejects the wisdom that comes from heaven, which James describes as being "first of all pure; then peace-loving, considerate, submissive, full of mercy and good fruit, impartial and sincere" (James 3:17).

This downward spiral continues. And because I am, like all humans, a creature of worship, I will find something or someone to be my focus. That could be self-gratification, my career, a relationship, or a cause such as worldwide acceptance of same-sex marriage. The consequence of this action is breathtakingly horrific and we read in verse 24: "So God abandoned them to do whatever shameful things their hearts desired."

Should we be surprised that once God removed His staying hand from them, the people chose to engage in sexual behaviour? Let us be perfectly clear: the people whom Paul refers to know God's truth, for people need to own something before they can trade it for something else. And verse 25 states that the people *"traded the truth about God for a lie"*. Are you ever tempted to exchange the truth you know for the lie you want to possess? (But afterwards, have you found the lie eventually takes possession of you?)

Thanksgiving is a defensive and offensive weapon

Thanksgiving is the key to maintaining our belief in a good God. A recent popular task on the social media site Facebook has been to state three things to be thankful for on a daily basis. It may not seem much of a task if your day has gone swimmingly. But if it has been a struggle to simply get out of bed and function, then to stop, assess, and declare three positives worthy of thanksgiving helps keep God central in our lives. We are not without a powerful enemy whose sole aim is to separate us from our Creator. In the Gospel of John, Jesus makes it clear: "The thief's purpose is to steal and kill and destroy. My purpose is to give them a rich and satisfying life" (John 10:10, NLT). Even on the worst of days, the most basic Facebook-type form of thanksgiving keeps us in sufficient touch with the life-giver who fills us with His own Holy Spirit.

Armed with the unshakeable truth that God is good, we can then develop a lifestyle of thanksgiving. Satan is keen to encourage discontent in all areas of our life and conveniently offers rather appealing solutions to that restlessness.

I know this from personal experience. It has not been easy for me these past thirty years, living as a single woman in a secular society that endorses the "if it feels good, do it" mentality, and in a Christian society that heavily promotes the nuclear family. In denying myself the option of making a home with another woman and yet not having transitioned into a place of heterosexual marriage, I have had to face some rather difficult consequences of my obedience to God. Denying myself the intimacy of relationship that I previously knew and enjoyed, not ever having had the chance to bear children, and entertaining the reality that I may never marry and could well grow old alone – all of these are opportunities for me to grow discontent and become bitter. On top of this, of course, there is now a strong Christian lobby declaring that we can have everything: God, a same-sex partner, and a happy ever after!

Bitterness

> Be careful that none of you fails to respond to the grace which God gives, for if he does there can very easily spring up in him a bitter spirit which is not only bad in itself but can also poison the lives of many others.
>
> **Hebrews 12:15**, J. B. PHILLIPS

Have you ever tried to remove the taproot of a dandelion? It sinks deep into the soil and thickens in breadth, which ensures the stability of the weed above, and requires a tremendous amount of hard labour to get it out of the ground. Bitterness, like a taproot, grows unseen. It derives its nutrients from a heart of unforgiveness that has been enriched by a combined sprinkling of "it's not fair" and "it's my right". Although it is critical to address the bitterness that may have arisen through past neglect or abuse at the hands of others, that is not the unforgiveness I am talking about here.

The unforgiveness I want to highlight requires me to ask you some questions:

- Are you harbouring unforgiveness toward God because of His statutes that forbid sexual relationships between those of the same gender, and only countenance sexual activity between a man and a woman within the confines of marriage?

- Are you possibly harbouring unforgiveness toward God because you have been faithfully obedient to His laws for the past fifteen years and have seemingly reaped only a harvest of disappointment and the pain of loneliness?

- Do you compare your life with Christians and non-Christians around you and shake your fist at God, yelling, "It's just not fair"?

Bitterness has friends

> Let there be no more resentment, no more anger or temper, no more violent self-assertiveness, no more slander and no more malicious remarks.
>
> **Ephesians 4:31**, J. B. PHILLIPS

If I am harbouring unforgiveness towards God for compelling me to be obedient in this area of sexuality, then I am in danger of inviting all of bitterness's friends into my heart. My growing resentment towards Him will feed feelings of anger expressed toward those who endorse God's teaching on this subject. I will begin to demand, perhaps only in my mind at first, that it is my right to love and be loved by another. After all, I cry, didn't God Himself say that it was not right for a man to live alone (Genesis 2:18)?

The root of bitterness continues to grow as I entertain those 2 per cent thoughts that God isn't fully good and doesn't fully love me and so I may attempt to justify my changing attitude by questioning the relevance of His laws in the twenty-first century. If I don't address these increasingly negative thoughts toward God I may, in time, even find like-minded people who will encourage me in my attempt to "unfollow" or even "unfriend" God and fulfil my pressing need and right for a loving, long-term relationship. Unchecked bitterness poisons our understanding of, and relationship with, our God, and that is why developing an attitude of thanksgiving is critical if we are to walk in grace and favour with our Lord.

A heart of thanksgiving

Thanklessness steers us away from the vertical relationship with God and sets us firmly on the horizontal plane, where we look for such things as identity, love, and justification outside of His prescribed guidelines. Thanksgiving, however, places us back in the framework of truth as we readily acknowledge that every good and perfect gift comes from above. It means that even if I don't understand why I haven't been given, at least to date, someone with whom I can grow old, thanksgiving re-affirms in me that God knows best and enables me to release those thoughts to Him.

Thanksgiving is a major weapon against the schemes of Satan who, as we discussed earlier, is determined to undermine the truth that God is good. Using this weapon of thanksgiving ensures that the enemy doesn't have a "foothold" (Ephesians 4:27, where the Greek *topos* means a "landing place") from which he can dig in and create a *stronghold*. So, as we read earlier in Psalm 100, full surety that God is good prompts a life of thanksgiving. But thanksgiving isn't an end in itself. It is the key that opens the gate to the courts of praise before leading the believer into the holy place of worship and on into the most holy place of true intimacy.

Being sure that at all times, and in every way, God is good is foundational in learning how to dwell contentedly in the land that the Lord has granted. Expressing gratitude is not an accessory to life but a fundamental weapon in our battle against the evil one. I conclude this chapter with a couple of verses from Colossians:

As you live this new life, we pray that you will be strengthened from God's boundless resources, so that you will find yourselves able to pass through any experience and endure it with courage. You will even be able to thank God in the midst of pain and distress because you are privileged to share the lot of those who are living in the light. For we must never forget that he rescued us from the power of darkness, and re-established us in the kingdom of his beloved Son, that is, in the kingdom of light. For it is by his Son alone that we have been redeemed and have had our sins forgiven.

Colossians 1:11–12, J. B. PHILLIPS

Section 4

How we view God and understand His sovereignty will determine our readiness to obey, irrespective of how we feel. Our attitude towards Him determines the potential depth of our relationship with Him.

Chapter 10

Privileged People

> But you are God's "chosen generation", his "royal priesthood", his "holy nation", his "peculiar people" – all the old titles of God's people now belong to you. It is for you now to demonstrate the goodness of him who has called you out of darkness into his amazing light. In the past you were not "a people" at all: now you are the people of God. In the past you had no experience of his mercy, but now it is intimately yours.
>
> 1 Peter 2:9–10, J. B. PHILLIPS

Good news, bad news

Imagine the scene in the Temple courts. Jesus is well into His third year of ministry and has built up quite a reputation as a teacher and miracle worker throughout Israel. On this particular occasion, He is talking to a group of people consisting not only of ordinary Jews but also of priests and Pharisees. Jesus turns to the religious people in the crowd:

"Do you want the good news or the bad news first?"

"Whatever You want, Rabbi, You choose."

"If you come to Me and repent of your sins, and believe that I am the Messiah, you will be broken."

The priests, elders, and scribes ponder the statement, look around at each other, shrug their shoulders and ask,

"OK, Rabbi, what's the good news?"

"That was the good news," says Jesus. And, looking intently into their faces, He continues. "Have you never read in the Scriptures:

'The stone the builders rejected has become the *capstone*; the Lord has done this, and it is marvellous in our eyes'? Therefore I tell you that the kingdom of God will be taken away from you and given to a people who will produce its fruit. He who falls on this stone will be broken to pieces, but he on whom it falls will be crushed…"

They looked for a way to arrest him…

Matthew 21:42–44, 46a, emphasis mine

Capstone or cornerstone?

Your translation of the Bible may have the word "cornerstone" instead of "capstone". Indeed, two translations that are very different in their approach, the New King James and *The Message*, both translate this Greek word as "cornerstone" rather than "capstone". Does it matter? Well, if you are in the building trade I would definitely say "yes" to that question. However, regarding Jesus, I believe that the difference in translation merely emphasizes the way in which we are fully covered by Christ.

The capstone is the centre stone in the top of an arch and, quite simply, if you remove the capstone, the arch will collapse. In the first chapter of Hebrews we read: "The Son is the radiance of God's glory and the exact representation of his being, sustaining all things by his powerful word" (verse 3). And in Colossians it is written of Jesus: "He is before all things, and in him all things hold together. And he is the head of the body, the church…" (Colossians 1:17–18a). From these passages we can be confident that Jesus is the centre stone who holds everything in place: without Him everything will collapse.

The cornerstone is the first stone in the foundations of any construction. It unites two sides of the building and determines the stability of the rest of the structure. Five hundred years before Christ, Zechariah prophesied: "From Judah will come the cornerstone" (Zechariah 10:4a). And centuries earlier, the prophet Isaiah spoke of Jesus as such: "See, I lay a stone in Zion, a tested stone, a precious cornerstone for a sure foundation; the one who trusts will never be dismayed" (Isaiah 28:16). After Jesus had returned to heaven, Peter wrote: "Now to you who believe, the stone is precious" (1 Peter 2:7a). And indeed it is, for whether we read the word "*capstone*" or "cornerstone", Scripture continually reminds us of the supremacy of Jesus.

There may be a number of issues in our life that we need to address if we are to bring wayward attractions or deep-rooted identity issues under Christ's Lordship. Be assured that it takes determination and commitment to live in obedience. In my early years of following Jesus, I can guarantee that I felt many things – but privileged was certainly not one of them. However, if we are intentionally choosing to live out of the vertical framework of loving God with our whole heart, mind, and strength, we can remain confident, even though it may at times feel as if the roof is caving in and the surrounding walls are crumbling on every side. With Jesus as both the capstone and the cornerstone, we can be certain that *Christ is still holding everything together.*

What is so good about being broken?

If asked what a relationship with Jesus offers, most of us could come up with a quick list of benefits such as salvation, healing, wholeness, joy, and peace. And yet, in the passage I quoted earlier from Matthew 21, Jesus not only fails to mention these rewards, but also tells the religious leaders that the result of following Him will be brokenness. Can this be right? Is brokenness part of God's "package deal" and if it is, why do we view it in such a negative light?

My very dear friend, Brad Sargent, was instrumental in enabling my first book *Out of Egypt* to be extricated from my head and onto the page. Although we are now thousands of miles apart, thanks to the miracle of the internet he is still able to offer morsels of magnificence towards this current writing project. Like me, Brad experienced same-sex attraction from an early age but, unlike me, he has always chosen not to act upon those feelings. In commenting on his journey, Brad writes:

> I define my identity as a Christian male, I choose to remain sexually abstinent, and I actively avoid pornography of all kinds as much as possible in our sex-saturated culture. This is the specific path I've chosen for four decades to deal with temptations toward same-sex activities. Some might say I'm suffering for nothing, but again, I'm not working from their paradigm. I see suffering as inevitable, perhaps even anguish as inevitable. But despair and futility are not. The pathway I have chosen is one I consider the way of the cross. It is a way that acknowledges, embraces, and redeems suffering to generate beauty in the midst of ashes. In postmodern terms, this is how I've constructed a life/lifestyle that embodies radical discipleship, as best I've come to understand that as having great freedom within biblical boundaries.

Brad's story is not full of bells, whistles, or ticker tape that often accompany testimonies. But he has faithfully and diligently allowed Jesus into the unseen and broken parts of his life. This has resulted not only in "great freedom within biblical boundaries", as Brad puts it, but an enormous legacy through his tireless work for the Kingdom that will only be fully recognized in glory.

Those of us who choose to lay down our attractions, orientation, and behaviours are privileged people because we recognize the importance of being pro-active in our sanctification process. If I fail to cooperate with the process, then even if I grit my teeth and am able to refrain from sinful behaviour, I will not find godly freedom and contentment in obedience alone. In fact, I may well lay seeds of resentment and bitterness toward God's chosen boundaries. Allowing Christ to make His home in us through His sanctifying work is the only way we can volitionally and joyfully lay down our own desires and plans, and take up His chosen plan for us.

True discipleship is anything but passive and it really behoves all believers to be far more than babes waiting for their next feed and burp. I truly believe that those who are successful in bringing their SSA to order are able to, by example, *lead* other Christians in this process. We are, together, called to *walk* through a lifelong sanctification process so that we can be image bearers of Jesus on this earth and, empowered by His Holy Spirit, shed His light and be His salt in this fallen world.

We are privileged to be heirs and co-heirs with Jesus Himself and to be the host of His Holy Spirit within. In order to live fully in that blessing, however, it is necessary for God to dismantle and rebuild. And, as everyone who has ever engaged in building or renovation work will attest to, it can be a long and messy process that often unearths previously unknown pleasant surprises in conjunction with some new challenges along the way. What has to be dismantled and rebuilt will be unique to every individual, but we can be sure that every area that prevents intimacy with the Father, affection toward the Son, and reliance on the Spirit will be on the list of things to do. It matters little how long we have been a Christian or how much we feel we have already surrendered. There is always some aspect of our life that our dear Lord will want to refine.

Broken now or crushed later

> He who falls on this stone will be broken to pieces, but he on whom it falls will be crushed.
>
> **Matthew 21:44**

Jesus isn't offering an easy option here, as both choices involve discomfort and pain. However, what is clear about this statement is that no one, whether a person believes in Him or not, will remain untouched by God. Accepting Christ as your Saviour now and letting Him break you of your old ways and remould you as a child of God, may well involve times of disquiet and hurt. But it is far more preferable to meeting Him at a later date as your Judge and being crushed beneath His righteous power.

> Whoever believes in him is not condemned, but whoever does not believe stands condemned already because he has not believed in the name of God's one and only Son.
>
> **John 3:18**

One may be tempted to ask, in offering such an unwelcome choice, is Jesus being fair? No one in their right mind wants to be broken to pieces. We may admit that there are one or two areas in our character that need a little "tweaking", but we rather like the way we are. *It's comfortable, it's familiar, and anyway, it's just the way I am,* we protest. Sadly, the Bible doesn't agree with such an assessment:

And have you forgotten that word of encouragement that addresses you as sons: "My son, do not make light of the Lord's discipline, and do not lose heart when he rebukes you, because the Lord disciplines those he loves, and he punishes everyone he accepts as a son."

Hebrews 12:5–7

No discipline seems pleasant at the time, but painful. Later on, however, it produces a harvest of righteousness and peace for those who have been trained by it.

Hebrews 12:11

As God's sons,[57] we are made co-heirs with Jesus and are the recipients of every spiritual blessing in Christ (Ephesians 1:3), but such blessing comes with responsibilities and one such task is to submit to the Lord's authority. Just as Jesus learned obedience through suffering (Hebrews 5:8), we too need to walk a similar path. To be crushed by God is to be left without hope, but to be broken by Him results in blessing. Those who yield to God's restraint enter into a deeper, more satisfying, relationship with Him. And increased intimacy with our heavenly Father produces hitherto unimagined peace and a fruitful life. Even a cursory glance at the spiritual giants of the Bible leaves a reader in no doubt that, before God released them into His service, He broke these men and women of character traits, sinful dispositions, and/or behaviours that hindered their walk with Him.

---

57 This is not a gender issue. As women, we need to accept and understand our role as sons of God, just as men have to accept and understand their role as the bride of Christ. Who said Christianity was straightforward? As a new believer, it was with some bewilderment that I realized I had to become a son in order to fully embrace my damaged female self!

182

Joseph, Moses, and Peter

At an early age, Joseph showed evidence of the gift he had been given to interpret dreams, but his lack of wisdom and humility brought trouble rather than blessing. Slavery, imprisonment, and separation from his family for over twenty years gave opportunity for Joseph to mature in character and gifting, thus preparing him to prosper under that mantle of leadership to which God had called him.

What did Joseph think of this time of refining? We can find the answer to that question in Genesis 41:52: he named his second son Ephraim, meaning "fruitful". He declared: "it is because God has made me fruitful in the land of my suffering." Joseph could look back and see purpose in his challenges that produced, ultimately, a time of prosperity and blessing.

God's hand was upon Moses from birth. Brought up by his Hebrew mother, yet enjoying the comfort of an Egyptian household, Moses was forced into exile due to his rash decision-making. Within a short timeframe, his life as a privileged Egyptian prince became a distant memory as Moses laboured under the role of a Midianite shepherd, an occupation despised by all Egyptians.

Forty years later, God deemed Moses to be broken of his independent spirit and rash decision-making, and considered him ready to be an obedient and trustworthy man of God. So, at the "tender" age of eighty years, Moses was released into a ministry of power and responsibility as he led God's people from a land of slavery into the land of blessing.

As we read earlier in the book, the apostle Peter had to have his self-confidence challenged and, ultimately, crushed in order to embrace a life of full dependence on God. Transformation from the enthusiastic "I can do that" mentality, to the thoughtful

"Jesus, you know all things" attitude enabled Peter to become the "Rock" and thus fulfil Christ's prophetic word to him right at the beginning (John 1:42).

Jesus leads the way

Without doubt, offering our life for the purpose of breaking, no matter how tenderly God may do it, is a daunting task. But in looking at Jesus' life, we can learn how to face the process of being broken and not feel shattered, of being disciplined and yet still feel loved, and of suffering yet still knowing God's reassuring presence. Although He was God, Jesus humbly accepted the limitations of being human so that He could *fully understand* our predicament. When unjustly accused of wrongdoing, Jesus offered forgiveness rather than retaliation. And, although entitled to sit on a throne, our Lord chose to kneel and wash feet, reminding us that every part of our life is important to Him. Though perfectly capable of making His own decisions, Jesus laid down that right in deference to God's will, and now encourages us to do the same. Instead of engineering a miraculous escape from the cross, Jesus experienced the pain of crucifixion, and He who is eternal endured an ignominious death on a wooden cross.

Jesus referred to Himself as the bread of life. We know that a loaf of bread feeds no one unless it has first been broken. From the point when Jesus was born as a bastard son – at least in the world's eyes – to His abandonment on the cross by God His Father, Jesus accepted everything that was placed upon Him. Was it fair? Was it deserved? Of course not, but Jesus allowed Himself to be broken so that we need never be crushed.

There's something about Mary

Mary and Martha lived with their brother, Lazarus, in a village called Bethany, located some two miles east of Jerusalem. Jesus certainly knew this little family unit and stayed with them on occasion. But it was while He was absent that Lazarus was taken ill and, despite the sisters sending word for Jesus to come quickly, their brother died. We pick up the story as Jesus eventually turns up at the village.

On his arrival, Jesus found that Lazarus had already been in the tomb for four days. Bethany was less than two miles from Jerusalem, and many Jews had come to Martha and Mary to comfort them in the loss of their brother. When Martha heard that Jesus was coming, she went out to meet him, but Mary stayed at home.

"Lord," Martha said to Jesus, "if you had been here, my brother would not have died. But I know that even now God will give you whatever you ask."

Jesus said to her, "Your brother will rise again."

Martha answered, "I know he will rise again in the resurrection at the last day.

Jesus said to her, "I am the resurrection and the life. The one who believes in me will live, even though they die; and whoever lives by believing in me will never die. Do you believe this?"

"Yes, Lord," she told him, "I believe that you are the Messiah, the Son of God, who is to come into the world."

After she had said this, she went back and called her sister Mary aside. "The Teacher is here," she said, "and is asking for you." When Mary heard this, she got up quickly and went to him. Now Jesus had not yet entered the village, but was still at the place where Martha had met him. When the Jews who had been with Mary in the house, comforting her, noticed how quickly she got up and went out, they followed her, supposing she was going to the tomb to mourn there.

When Mary reached the place where Jesus was and saw him, she fell at his feet and said, "Lord, if you had been here, my brother would not have died."

When Jesus saw her weeping, and the Jews who had come along with her also weeping, he was deeply moved in spirit and troubled. "Where have you laid him?" he asked.

"Come and see, Lord," they replied.

Jesus wept.

Then the Jews said, "See how he loved him!"

John 11:17–36

There is much to consider in this passage but I want to highlight verses 21 and 32b because they tell us that both Martha and Mary greeted Jesus with the same charge: "Lord, if you had been here, my brother would not have died." Interestingly, these two sentences, although verbally similar, provoked a very different response in Jesus. In reaction to Martha's statement Jesus engaged in a theological discussion. But in response to Mary's assertion, Jesus went to the tomb of His friend Lazarus and wept. If you were experiencing the loss of someone dear to you or you were addressing a particularly difficult area in your life, would you want Jesus to engage in a theological discussion, or would you want Him to sit with you and weep?

Jesus' different responses to the two sisters were not some random comments that could have easily been delivered the other way round: weeping with Martha and discussing the theological implications of the resurrection with Mary. So why does He react so differently to each one?

What is very clear in verse 5 of this chapter is that Jesus *loved* both of the sisters as well as their brother Lazarus. There is never an indication that Jesus had preference for one sister over another, and we know from a general reading of the Scriptures that such a preference would not be in keeping with the character of God as revealed in Christ. God does not show favouritism (Acts 10:34; Romans 2:11). We can conclude, therefore, that Jesus' response to each woman reflected the *depth* of relationship He had with each one.

Bethany Life

The village of Bethany was a well-known stop-off point on the pilgrim's road from Galilee in the north, where Jesus lived, to the city of Jerusalem. During His three-year ministry, and perhaps even beforehand, Jesus spent time in this village and in the house of Martha, Mary, and Lazarus before travelling on to Jerusalem. We read that even when He was teaching in Jerusalem, Jesus sometimes left the city and walked the two miles to Bethany in order to spend the night there before returning to Jerusalem the next day (see Matthew 21:17; Mark 11:11). The time He spent with this family of siblings gave ample opportunity to nurture a deep and trusting friendship with all three.

We do not know if the sisters had witnessed any miracles first hand, but they were certainly recipients of Jesus' teachings. Although Jesus chastizes Martha at one point (Luke 10) for putting her service ahead of spending time with Him, it is clear that Martha must have been listening at many other times, for her understanding of Christ's teaching and intentions was very clear. Given their sincere relationship with Jesus, therefore, it was understandable for the sisters to send word to their friend when Lazarus became gravely ill. Jesus may or may not have been in the region of Perea (east of the Jordan river) at this time, but it is clear from the timing of events later on in the story that He was no more than one day's walk away from the family.

Expectations and response

What were the sisters to expect? What would you have expected Jesus, your dear friend and miracle worker, to do? At the very least, I would have wanted Him to get the next donkey back to Bethany or speak healing to Lazarus from a distance as He had done to the servant of the Roman centurion (Matthew 8:5–13).

What did Jesus do? He got the message about Lazarus's illness, said something obscure about bringing glory to God, and then stayed where He was for two more days. Given their relationship, perhaps what is most surprising is that Jesus didn't even bother to send any message of comfort back to Martha and Mary. Lazarus must have died soon after the sisters sent the message, because he had been in the tomb for four days by the time Jesus sauntered up the road towards the village. How would you have felt as you looked out of the window and saw the one man you believed in, trusted in, and loved finally turn up? Angry? Frustrated? Confused? Betrayed?

Both Martha and Mary believed wholeheartedly that Jesus was the Messiah, the Son of God who had come to bring them salvation and eternal life. The women may not have understood why Jesus didn't turn up earlier, or heal their brother from a distance, or at least send them a message of comfort. But they did not convert their lack of understanding into anger or withdrawal. They recognized the need to submit to God's ways and His timing, even when they were in pain, or didn't understand the situation, or couldn't see a great future ahead. They believed the Scripture in Isaiah that reads: "'For my thoughts are not your thoughts, neither are your ways my ways,' declares the Lord. 'As the heavens are higher than the earth, so my ways are higher than your ways and my thoughts than your thoughts'" (Isaiah 55:8–9).

Even in submission, however, Martha responded to type and ran to meet Jesus on the road. "'Lord,' Martha said to Jesus, 'if you had been here, my brother would not have died. But I know that even now God will give you whatever you ask'" (John 11:21–22). Martha fixed her eyes on one thing, and that was an answer to her problems. Right now she was not interested in Jesus as a person or a dear friend, but as a means to making everything better. Because Martha's emotions seem disconnected with her head, she derives no comfort when Jesus says: "Your brother will rise again." Jesus was meaning today, very soon, within the hour. But dear Martha could only hear with her head and answered: "I know he will rise again in the resurrection at the last day."

Martha, in agreement with the teaching of the Pharisees, was theologically sound but had not grasped the living word that Jesus was offering. In her desire for a solution, Martha appears to have heard only what Jesus said and not *how* He spoke to her.

In contrast, Mary responds to the request of Jesus and hurries along the road to where He is still standing. "When Mary reached the place where Jesus was and saw him, she fell at his feet and said, 'Lord, if you had been here, my brother would not have died'" (John 11:32). In the past, Mary had sat at Jesus' feet, listening to Him teach. She had knelt at His feet and worshipped. And here, now, she fell at His feet and wept. Mary didn't ask Jesus why He had let her brother die, although she must have been puzzled by the events. Neither did she ask for a change in her circumstances even though I'm sure she would have welcomed them. Mary didn't even ask for Jesus to make her feel better, although I'm certain she would have embraced some respite from her grief. Instead, even in this time of great trauma, Mary did what she always did: she worshipped.

The word "worship" means to "prostrate oneself in homage". It is a term that describes the action of a person bowing down before someone great. It is a sign of total humility and devotion. It is the surrender of our thoughts, our desires, and our ways before the King of Kings and the Lord of Lords. Worship doesn't require understanding, but it does require submission. And that can only come out of a growing relationship with Jesus. In Mary of Bethany, we see how a life of worshipping, sitting at Christ's feet, and listening to Him, equipped her to face trauma and loss in the same spirit.

The bigger picture

Right now, you may be engaged in a personal battle with online pornography, or doing your level best not to succumb to the draw of a relationship that you know will result in emotional enmeshment. It is possible that the last thing you feel right now is privileged. But may I encourage you that you are walking in the footsteps of some mighty men and women of God who have all had to face their frailties as part of their journeying into a deeper relationship with Him? Is it possible to lift your head and see your situation from a different angle?

In July 1945 *The Coventry Evening Telegraph* published a short piece by C.S. Lewis entitled "Meditations in a Toolshed."[58] In this article Lewis described standing in a shed that was completely dark save for one beam of light and illuminated

58 Originally published in *The Coventry Evening Telegraph* (17 July 1945); reprinted in *God in the Dock* (Eerdmans, 1970), pp. 212–215.

specks of floating dust. All else, he noted, remained in the dark. Then Lewis changed position and placed himself so that the beam shone into his eyes and, once he had adjusted to the change, the author noted the stark difference in his outlook. He no longer saw the toolshed or even the beam itself but was able to look along the shaft out through the crack in the door and beyond his current location. He saw leaves, sky, and eventually the sun itself some 149 million kilometres away.

The question I want to ask you is this: are you looking at your current struggles with certain facets of same-sex attraction in isolation, or are you looking at them from within the framework of truth?

With Jesus as your capstone and your cornerstone, you can take heart that He will keep you from falling as you yield your heart, mind, soul, and strength to Him. Using C. S. Lewis's analogy, I encourage you to stand in our Lord's beam and focus your eyes out through the gap in the door, past the swaying trees, beyond the sun, and onto the Creator of all things. In so doing, you will be able to keep your current struggles in perspective and see them as part of your ongoing sanctification process – not as a stumbling block, but as a springboard towards greater intimacy with the Father.

> The Lord will guide you always; he will satisfy your needs in a sun-scorched land and will strengthen your frame. You will be like a well-watered garden, like a spring whose waters never fail. Your people will rebuild the ancient ruins and will raise up the age-old foundations; you will be called Repairer of Broken Walls, Restorer of Streets with Dwellings.
>
> Isaiah 58:11–12

Chapter 11

She Did What She Could

Oblivious to the driving rain and unrelenting wind, little Jenny (not her real name) stood to my left, hanging on every word I spoke. Despite her heavy boots, her oversize stick, and a games skirt that reached her knees, nothing was going to deter Jenny from learning all she could about the game of hockey. It was 1980 and I was teaching physical education at a girls' boarding school in England. And from that first lesson until I left five years later, Jenny never lost her enthusiasm for sport. It wasn't as though she had natural ability in any of the disciplines and there were many girls who were far more talented and successful than Jenny. Yet, thirty-five years later, Jenny is one of the few girls I can remember by name.

She was never going to earn a living from playing sport, nor was she going to represent her country or county. But that never dampened her desire to participate wholeheartedly in whatever she was told to do. Unlike some of the students who were blessed with abundant natural ability but lacked interest, the ever-smiling little Jenny was a joy to teach and a pleasure to be around. I never expected Jenny to achieve the skill level of some of the girls in her class and I never demanded it from her. All I ever wanted from my pupils was for them to apply themselves wholeheartedly to the lesson and to fulfil their potential, however high or low that may have been. The end-of-term report at this particular school required the teacher not only to make a written statement but also to give each girl a grade for achievement and a second grade for effort. Needless to say, when it came to the box marked "effort", Jenny never failed to achieve the top grade.

The anointing of Jesus

While he was in Bethany, reclining at the table in the home of a man known as Simon the Leper, a woman came with an alabaster jar of very expensive perfume, made of pure nard. She broke the jar and poured the perfume on his head. Some of those present were saying indignantly to one another, "Why this waste of perfume? It could have been sold for more than a year's wages and the money given to the poor." And they rebuked her harshly. "Leave her alone," said Jesus. "Why are you bothering her? She has done a beautiful thing to me. The poor you will always have with you, and you can help them any time you want. But you will not always have me. She did what she could. She poured perfume on my body beforehand to prepare for my burial. Truly I tell you, wherever the gospel is preached throughout the world, what she has done will also be told, in memory of her."

Mark 14:3–9

In the previous chapter, we recognized that time spent in Christ's company is not wasted. Mary's intimate relationship with Jesus enabled her to press into Him even though she was grieving the loss of her precious brother. Mary did not accuse Jesus of being uncaring or heartless because He failed to respond favourably to the sisters' request for help. Her relationship with Jesus went far deeper than relying on His actions to define their bond.

There is so much that we do not know about this family of Martha, Mary, and Lazarus, but we do know that they were three siblings sharing the same house. It seems that none of them, at least during the time of Jesus' ministry, were married and there is no hint of any children present in the house. Unless their hospitality was actually a business, not dissimilar to a budget hotel (they were on the pilgrim route to Jerusalem), we see no visible income generated by the family. And yet Mary has in her possession a vial of expensive nard worth, in today's terms, about £35,000 or US$55,000 which would certainly keep her from poverty and at least offer some security.

If she felt she had to spend it then, as was pointed out to her, there were many reasonable avenues of action she could have taken. She could have divided the money sensibly, keeping enough for her and giving the rest to good causes, and in so doing she would have offered an acceptable face of worship and gained the approval of those present.

Reckless abandoned worship

But Mary had sat in Jesus' company for too long and had listened to His voice and captured His heartbeat for life. She had experienced forgiveness, love, and approval, and found an identity in Christ that overrode any other claim on her existence. Mary knew the truth about Jesus and, by pouring this expensive perfume over the head of her Beloved, this woman declared openly that Christ was her provision now and her security in the future. Her reckless, abandoned worship prompted the single voice of Jesus' approval, thus silencing the jarring yell of her detractors. In Mark 14:6 in *The Message* we read:

> But Jesus said, "Let her alone. Why are you giving her
> a hard time? She has just done something wonderfully
> significant for me."

Mary had not preached the finest sermon ever heard, nor had she written a best-selling book that resulted in thousands of repenting souls coming to salvation. But she incited a favourable response from her Lord because Mary loved Him with her whole heart, mind, soul, and strength. Her worship was something wonderfully significant to Jesus, just as our worship is equally something wonderfully significant to Him. When we offer the extravagant gift of our inner being, even the cracked, chipped, and broken bits, we are doing what we can, and that will always elicit a favourable response from our Lord.

The detractors

Acts of abandoned worship will inevitably bring detractors from all quarters. One expects voices of indignation from society in general, simply because those without God's Spirit are incapable of understanding what is happening (Romans 8:7). However, it is often difficult to live with criticism from fellow believers. There was nothing reasonable about Mary's act of worship and her behaviour was certainly void of any forward planning. But, critically, it was totally acceptable to Christ.

The subject of homosexuality is divisive inside and outside of the church. Individuals who vocalize that homosexual behaviour is incompatible with biblical teaching, and not only cease to act on their impulses and attractions but also choose to seek help in that area, can have their very testimony besmirched by believers and non-believers alike. They are dismissed as phoney or deluded and completely out of touch with the twenty-first century. But these godly men and women, many of whom are still addressing very real issues, such as early sexual abuse or abandonment, have had to face the added complication of more "enlightened" Christians offering them solace within the boundaries of a monogamous, same-sex, faith-based relationship.

The widow in the Temple

It is during the difficult, challenging times when we need to know that God notes our sacrificial steps of obedience, no matter how small or feeble.

> Sitting across from the offering box, he was observing how the crowd tossed money in for the collection. Many of the rich were making large contributions. One poor widow came up and put in two small coins – a measly two cents. Jesus called his disciples over and said, "The truth is that this poor widow gave more to the collection than all the others put together. All the others gave what they'll never miss; she gave extravagantly what she couldn't afford – she gave her all."
>
> Mark 12:41–44, *The Message*

> For the eyes of the Lord range throughout the earth to strengthen those whose hearts are fully committed to him.
>
> 2 Chronicles 16:9a

This is exactly what Jesus was doing – looking to and fro – when He noticed the widow across the Court of Women. The Temple treasury was located within this court and was accessible to all but Gentiles and unclean women. It was also the main thoroughfare for those men permitted to enter deeper into other Temple courts. And yet, it was in this crowded, bustling place that Jesus noticed the solitary widow. The gift that she was giving was not the obligatory Temple tax, but a freewill offering beyond what was expected. In truth, what the widow gave had little monetary value and it certainly would not have added to the cash required to upkeep such a splendid building. But all of that was of no concern to Jesus and I am reminded of God's directive to Samuel when he is looking for the new king of Israel.

> But the Lord said to Samuel, "Do not consider his
> appearance or his height, for I have rejected him.
> The Lord does not look at the things people look
> at. People look at the outward appearance, but
> the Lord looks at the heart."
>
> 1 Samuel 16:7

People milling around in the Court of Women may have been impressed with the actions of the rich, but in Jesus' Kingdom the widow surpassed the rich people in her giving: she gave from her devotion to God and it was, therefore, fully acceptable to Him. Indeed, Jesus was so buoyed up by her actions that He called the disciples who were scattered around the court to Him so that He could tell them the importance of her gift: the widow did what she could and Jesus took notice.

Kara's story

I have borne witness to some amazing transformations during the past thirty years and I suppose none are more dramatic than when a transgendered person, prompted by God's Spirit, chooses to embrace and live out of their birth gender. I have even known a handful of people actually undergo further surgery in order to rectify previous work that they have had performed on their bodies.

But not all outward expressions of inner change are that easy to spot and, sometimes, the main change has been in disposition and attitude that barely registers externally. Yet this inner work is critical for us to continue to dwell contentedly within God's framework of truth. This is so of my American friend, Kara. I have known Kara for three years now and she has written out part of her story below.

I did not think about being gay while I was growing up because in those days such things were not talked about openly and I didn't even realize the scope of what was going on in my life. It has been over thirty years since I gave my heart to Jesus and began to work through the process of life. At least fifteen of those years had something to do with working through same-sex attraction or emotional dependency, but I found out that working through lesbianism was just a stretch of the road in the bigger road map of God's purposes for my life... and that is – as *The Message* version says in Ephesians 4:22–24 – to "take on an entirely new life – a God-fashioned life, a life renewed from the inside and working itself into your conduct as God accurately reproduces his character in [me]".

There are some commonalities in the histories of women who identify as lesbian, and except for childhood sexual abuse, many of those factors were present in my life. But I've come to learn that many women can experience these same root issues and not be same-sex attracted, and I've come to the conclusion that homosexuality is just part of the Fall, and that is where some of us ended up for whatever reason. In the mid-1980s, even though I had been a Christian for a few years, I still did not understand why I or anyone else was gay. This was a great mystery to me and none of my lesbian friends ever talked about it. We just were. A short time after that I was able to get some books through Exodus International – a ministry for those affected by homosexuality – which explained a lot of what I had experienced, but there were still things I didn't understand about my life. There were four specific things I was able to identify:

- *I always wanted to be a boy.*
- *I hated my mom.*
- *I had a tremendous fear of femininity.*
- *I had a skewed perception of males and was accepted by males as "one of the guys".*

[For] as long as I [can] remember, I wanted to be a boy. I remember praying to God to change me into a boy and I believed that some day I would wake up and physically be a boy. The greatest day of my fifth-grade life was when I got a football uniform [UK – kit] for Christmas. Some of my wanting to be a boy might have been that boys got to do everything and girls got left out. I loved sports and was better than most of the boys [in my class], but where I lived in the 1960s, girls were not allowed to play organized sports.

As early as third grade, I had emotional crushes on female teachers and girls who were three to six years older than me; I was infatuated with them. By the time I was in seventh grade, those older girls had graduated but I continued to have a crush on one of my female teachers the last three years of high school. I also began to notice that I wanted to be close physically with some of my female friends instead of the boys, although I didn't think of the possibility of being gay because in the 1970s, such things were not talked about except in whispers and gossip… and besides, there was one boy I really liked.

During junior high I began to hate my mom. My parents were very good to us and we didn't grow up in a physically abusive home. Many times my parents sacrificed so that my sister and I could have material things, but my mom and I never connected emotionally. I felt I could never share my heart and the times I did try, I felt she thought my emotions were stupid. I know that many times rejection is a perceived thing in a child's mind, but that doesn't make it any less real. So I totally cut myself off from her emotionally and began to search for any female who would affirm and understand me.

Teenage years

In high school, my whole identity became wrapped up in my talents and abilities and what car I drove. The car of choice for me was a muscle car – not a feminine type of car at all. The ironic thing was I thought the boys would like me if I drove a cool car, but that car actually turned out to be a chick magnet when I was at college. Because I loved sports at a time when women's sports were not that accepted, I was somewhat of a misfit and often received a lot of ridicule for wearing boys' sportswear, mostly from the girls.

The only time any guy showed interest in me was when he was drunk and even though I tried to be feminine by doing make-up, steam rollers, and dressing appropriately, it still wasn't enough to interest a guy romantically. Many times I was made fun of when I tried to do things like a girl and I became fearful of risking any feminine action. Dates and proms just did not exist for me. I kept asking myself what was wrong with me. Am I that ugly, that weird? Just because I liked sports and guy things, did that make me unacceptable as a female? The image I had of myself as a female continued to deteriorate.

College years

My freshman year at college was a turning point in my decision to pursue a lesbian identity. I made the team and became a manager for the university basketball team. I really liked these women and I sensed something was different about some of them: these were the women I wanted as friends. They loved sports and motorcycles and all the other things I liked. These were the women jocks on campus, and now I was a solid part of their group and at last I felt I had come home; this was where I belonged. I was loved and accepted for who I was… for what I felt was the first time in my life and from that point on, I no longer cared about being accepted by men. I was part of the lesbian community for the next five years.

While growing up, I went to church every Sunday but did not have a personal relationship with Jesus. I even got involved in a Bible study with real born-again Christians who were in Campus Crusade and Navigators. But because I didn't have a relationship with Jesus, it was easy to dump the Bible studies, and it seemed the basketball team was having a whole lot more fun than the Christians. While I was in college I remember sitting in front of the TV thinking that if I died I would go to hell. I did not care! I had another god – a woman lover. My emotional and physical needs were being met and I didn't care what God thought about it. After college, I moved to another state to live with my girlfriend. Even after that relationship ended, I was not unhappy in my identity and was not even thinking of God or of trying to change.

A godly prompt

But I was walking in the woods one day and had a thought that I needed to check out this Jesus "thing" again, which was strange because I didn't know one Christian in my community and no one was chasing me with a big black Bible. I lived in the woods with a bunch of wonderful women who drove motorcycles, Jeeps, and trucks; who cut down trees with chainsaws; and who shot porcupines that chewed our tires. And I'm still friends with all of these women.

I cannot tell you the day or even the month thirty years ago that I sat in the pastor's office and asked Jesus into my life, but I know something in my heart changed that day. As I began to read the Bible for the first time, I believed that the Holy Spirit was showing me that lesbianism was no longer an option for my life.

I argued with God for at least a year that it was not fair that, if I wanted to be in a sexual relationship, I had to be married to a man. I was still attracted to women and I had to work through some pretty big emotional dependency issues. Loneliness was a big hurdle to overcome and my gay friends would run from me because I told them they needed to turn or burn. (I eventually figured out that method wasn't the best approach.) I didn't trust people at church with my secret of lesbianism, and at that time being gay was about the most shameful thing you could be. But I had a great cat that was a wonderful source of comfort and I remember saying to the cat one day, "What would I do without you?" Two days later I accidently ran over the cat, but it was during all those hard times that Jesus proved His faithfulness and, thirty years later, He is still showing me His grace.

The ongoing journey

I've met people who think that when someone who is gay or lesbian gets saved, it is a simple matter of praying, reading the Bible, going to church, [and] meeting someone from the opposite sex who is cute. Nothing could be further from the truth. Leaving homosexuality is like moving to another planet.

I don't think being straight was ever the goal. Understanding the bigger picture God had for my life and just trying to grow in Christ was the goal. It was through deepening my relationship with Him that I began to notice subtle changes in my thoughts and attractions. These changes were like the parable in Mark 4 about the growing seed. "And Jesus said, 'The Kingdom of God is as if a man should scatter seed on the ground, and should sleep by night and rise by day, and the seed should sprout and grow, but he himself does not know how.'"

Someone has said that change happens one good decision at a time. As I began to try to be obedient to what I felt God was saying, then I would wake up some mornings and my thoughts about certain things would just be different; I don't have a clue how God does that.

Unfinished business

Even years after my conversion, the reason why I wanted to be a boy was still a great mystery to me. However, I have found that God is a God of individuality and He wants to minister to those very private and special places that all of us guard in our hearts. He chooses the time to reveal what He wants to show us. Because of my school experiences and certain attitudes toward men conveyed to me by my family, I had a tremendous fear of femininity. Airline attendants were absolutely the most terrifying creatures on the earth and I couldn't even look at them. I felt like if I got up to use the restroom in the plane that I was bothering them and even if I was freezing there was no way I was going to ask them for a blanket.

Then during a time of prayer some fourteen years ago, the Holy Spirit showed me that because of some family history, the struggle for my gender identity began in the womb. As Genesis 25 describes Esau as red-colored from struggling with Jacob in Rebekah's womb, I saw myself red with rage, kicking and screaming, wearing black hi-top tennis shoes and pink frilly socks. This picture revelation continued and I saw myself as a toddler in diapers, walking hand in hand with Jesus.

In sixth grade, the most torturous thing my mother could ever do to me was make me wear fishnet stockings and patent leather shoes, especially as my personal idea of being dressed up was a paisley western shirt, boys' pants with a big western belt buckle, and the outfit completed with cowboy boots. But in this revelation, I saw myself with Jesus and I was wearing a white dress, white fishnet stockings, and patent leather shoes. Jesus gave me a big red heart filled with chocolate. God had not yet finished, because I then saw myself as a woman dancing with Jesus and I was wearing a long white dress, pearls, white gloves, and white shoes – and was feeling totally comfortable with being there. Jesus was wearing a tux, not a robe.

Acceptance

This was great, but I wondered when the black tennis shoe was going to go away and I would turn into a pink frilly sock. At a ministry training course some three years later I shared this dilemma with our small group leader because it really bothered me. Of course, much to my dismay, there was one very feminine woman in our group and on the very last day of the training, she approached me. This woman told me that she believed the Holy Spirit showed her that the black shoe was just as important as the pink frilly sock and that the black shoe represented strength and grace, just as a ballet dancer needs strength and grace in her feet and legs. At worship that night I saw myself dancing with Jesus and under the long white dress I was wearing black hi-top tennis shoes and pink frilly socks. Jesus just winked and smiled, and from that moment I knew I could be confident with who I was created to be.

Change?

You see, I didn't exactly fit in with what our society considers feminine and I still don't. I didn't have the same interests as many women in the church, and I still don't. That was really problematic in the past and I used to be on a mission of what I perceived to be a pink frilly sock. But, after that night, I experienced deep internal transformation: I was no longer fearful of feminine women. In fact, one of my dearest friends is a retired flight attendant! God hasn't stopped His transformative work because, even now, when a feminine woman accepts me for me, it brings yet another measure of healing to that once very damaged sense of the feminine.

I read in Psalm 33:13–15: "The Lord looks from heaven; He sees all the sons of men. From the place of His dwelling He looks on all the inhabitants of the earth. He fashions their hearts individually; He considers all their works." (NKJV) When I read that verse that day, I was set free to accept that God created me to be unique and that is OK. My main concern in life is not that I prove I have changed, because people are going to think what they are going to think. My concern in life is: Am I being obedient for today? Change happens… one good decision at a time.

One good decision at a time

Has God given you an idea of the man or woman He is calling you to be? I don't particularly mean a significant change in your outward demeanor, although for some that may be the case. I am talking here about possessing true freedom in Christ. It is easy to look at the full picture and think that the journey towards wholeness is just too long and too difficult, and end up dissatisfied with one's lot.

In chapter 5 we looked at the situation facing the tribe of Dan and their refusal to claim the land that God had given them. Instead of believing God's promise, "I will give you every place where you set your foot" (Joshua 1:3), the Danites chose to look at their current circumstances and potential difficulties, and remain huddled together in the foothills instead of faithfully travelling west and confronting their well-armed enemy when the occasion arose.

We know that by failing to appropriate God's promise, a number of Danites travelled north. They seized land that was never meant to be theirs and ultimately succumbed to a lifestyle far removed from the ordinances of God. The remainder of the Danites fared little better, and their refusal to take God at His word resulted in their assimilation into the local culture and customs until this tribe ceased to exist.

No one is suggesting that taking this ground is easy, but, as Kara stated, change is made by making one good decision at a time. Pastor and author Bill Johnson writes:

> This is the essence of faith – not intellectual assent to truths; but the practical trust we express in God based on who we know Him to be through our relationship with Him. We express that trust when we choose to listen to Him in the midst of our circumstances more than any other voice and then respond to our circumstances in light of what He has said. [59]

---

59 Bill Johnson, *Strengthen Yourself in the Lord: How to Release the Hidden Power of God in Your Life*, Shippensburg, PA: Destiny Image, 2007, Kindle edition, p. 40.

Chapter 12

The Danger of Distraction

Let be and be still, and know (recognize and understand) that I am God.

Psalm 46:10, AMP

diting photographs on my computer engrosses me for long periods of time. Hours go by before I stop and realize that I am hungry, thirsty, or that I'm actually about to experience deep vein thrombosis. But if I am staring at a blank screen and need to write a teaching or blog, then I can be distracted by a multitude of stimuli, each of which, no matter how small, demands my undivided attention.

Someone once wrote that we are a society of the half-read page and I'm guilty as charged, for I skim through blogs and articles and, if not gripped after reading the first two sentences, continue scrolling until something else catches my eye. I'm convinced that the various forms of social media foster and indulge a societal malaise of Attention Deficit Hyperactivity Disorder (ADHD).

Prioritize

Making time to just sit with the Lord is a challenge. For a number of people, God has been reduced to snatched morsels of Scripture eaten on the run, or a diet of snacks provided by this month's Bible notes. Other people's quiet time may consist of little more than playing Christian CDs or listening to Christian radio on their drive into work in the morning. I recognize that there are seasons in life, such as while parenting very young children, when this may be all that can be achieved.

But, when it comes to the larger life picture, there is no shortcut method to becoming one of Christ's disciples.

In Psalm 46:10, the Hebrew verb *raphah* not only means to "be still", but is also used elsewhere in Scripture as "to sink", "relax", "sink down", "let drop", or "withdraw". The implication in this word *raphah* is that God is calling us to a whole-body experience, rather than just a pause in proceedings. The Amplified Bible's translation offers three areas that need to be addressed:

- "Let be" (stop what you are thinking or planning or are mindful of)
- "be still" (stop all of your activity and quiet yourself)
- "and know". (The Hebrew word used here is *yada* and is used to describe a very intimate form of knowing as well as being translated as "to perceive and see", "find out and discern", "to discriminate", "distinguish", or "know by experience".)

Did you notice that all three are actually "action verbs" – they require us to choose to do something – despite how they might appear to be passive because they instruct us to slow down? Distractions can present as much the preferred option, but we need to be intentional and choose to engage in these three actions if we want to grow in relationship with the Lord.

What is a distraction?

Distractions can be quite hard to recognize. I have come to the conclusion that, as a general rule, while we may be tempted *to* sin, we are distracted *by* things that are not necessarily bad as such but are just not beneficial at that particular time. Living in a persistent state of distraction may well be indicative of a fear of intimacy and can, if not addressed, prove detrimental to our long-term Christian walk.

Distraction can occur in every aspect of life. For instance, a new gardener may have every intention of tending his vegetable plot for a few hours every Saturday, but is distracted by a succession of visitors or family invites. The business person may target the gym after work three times a week, but deadlines for the next day take priority. Commonly, many Christians determine to get up thirty minutes earlier every morning to read their Bible, but several late nights involving some difficult pastoral issue take their toll and eventually scupper the idea.

Little things can eat into the best of plans and we can end up out of sorts with ourselves for not being better organized or self-disciplined. Or, they can divert our attention in deceptive ways such as we are still accomplishing something, but the quality of it is not what it could or should be. This equally common form of distraction entraps us in mediocrity: getting so carried along by what is *good* that we fail to notice or embrace what is *best*.

Aiming for maturity

Not all distractions are short term or easily rectified.

> The seed that fell among thorns stands for those who hear, but as they go on their way they are choked by life's worries, riches and pleasures, and they do not mature.
>
> Luke 8:14

"Worries, riches and pleasures" rather sums up Western society in the twenty-first century and today's Christians are not immune from nurturing such thorns in their own patch of land. Jesus points out the danger of allowing those three areas to determine our thoughts, words, and deeds. At salvation we are reconciled to God and He puts His Spirit in us as a seal of this new covenantal relationship, encouraging conformity to His ways and empowering us to grow in godliness (Philippians 2:13). Much as we may wish instant transformation, our cooperation as believers is required in this sanctification process until, finally, we see Jesus face to face and, unbelievably, become just like Him (1 John 3:2). Such is the journey for every young and carnal believer.

The problem, says Jesus, is that these three thorns – worries, riches and pleasures – have one purpose in life and that is to choke life out of the believer, preventing his or her maturation in the Lord and thus inhibiting fruitfulness. What does this mean in the context of same-sex attraction?

Worries

Apart from general life worries there is a certain pattern of concern that besets men and women seeking to bring their sexuality and attractions under the Lordship of Christ.

- Can I live without sex?
- Who do I talk to about my feelings?
- What happens if I fall in love with someone?
- What happens if I don't fall in love with someone?
- Will I grow old alone?
- Will my church understand?
- Can I live without being special to someone?
- Am I strong enough to do this?
- What if I fail?

These and many other thoughts and concerns can really weigh a believer down and crowd out the joy of God's salvation message.

Riches

Few Christians, whatever their background, escape the need to create sufficient income to pay the bills and feed and clothe themselves. However, a man or woman addressing their SSA may face costs that are a direct result of their commitment to biblical teaching. This often means that it is a lack of money rather than the pursuit of money that can distract a believer.

For instance – and this is certainly not the prerogative of those who are SSA but may be necessary for any Christian man or woman seeking to follow the Lord – it is not unusual for an individual to find it necessary to leave town or an area in order to remove his or herself from the immediate temptation of sexual sin or relational dependency issues. Over the years I have known both men and women leave good jobs and relocate elsewhere not only to remove them from temptation, but to put themselves in areas where a ministry relevant to their needs is located. Taking minimum wage or low-paid jobs and renting a room has been the price they have paid in order to pursue their commitment to Christ.

An unmarried heterosexual couple who come to Christ can easily rectify that state by getting married. But what of the gay couple who are in a civil partnership or married? What if they are parents? What if they have a joint mortgage on their home? Apart from the emotional, spiritual, and physical challenges that arise in such a situation, the financial cost can be staggering and, again, distract the attention of the godliest of believers.

Pleasures

This particular brier can attack a gay-identified or gay-oriented believer on so many levels. As a new convert, I just didn't feel capable of saying "no" to sexual sin. So I chose to stop investing time and energy in old relationships and the bars and clubs that had been my social scene for so many years. The problem was that I didn't have anyone or anything to replace what I had walked away from.

The people in the church I was attending were friendly enough, but it takes a long while to create and foster meaningful friendships. The non-disclosure over my still-held gay identity and ongoing attractions understandably hindered the development of any such relationships, and so I experienced a very difficult couple of years in relational wilderness. As a form of solace, I would replay scenarios in my head of "the good old days" when I smiled and laughed and generally had fun. The worse my present reality seemed, the more positive my memories of the past appeared to be, and it was very hard not to resent the seemingly poor Christian hand I had been dealt for moving into the future.

Some of my friends straddled both the Christian and the gay world. This didn't necessarily mean sexual sin was committed, but by just hanging out in gay-affirming locations, my friends would feed that need to belong. However necessary it seemed at the time, it was clear that their enjoyment was rarely guilt-free and many ended up being increasingly discontent with this dual existence. Unfortunately, no small number ended up returning to at least a gay-affirming and sometimes even sexually active way of life.

Pleasure and rights

One of the most well-known sentences in the world is in the United States' Declaration of Independence. Written and enacted in 1776, this document announced that the thirteen American colonies would no longer be part of the British empire but instead would function independently of Great Britain. The famous sentence reads:

We hold these truths to be self-evident, that all men are created equal, that they are endowed by their Creator with certain unalienable Rights that among these are Life, Liberty and the pursuit of Happiness.

The document was so well written and profound in nature that it has since been used as a template for numerous other human rights documents. As it was written by men who feared God, I can only presume that their intention was that "Life, Liberty, and the pursuit of Happiness" would be subject to the primacy of Scripture. But today's Western society seemingly seeks the pursuit of happiness above all other things and much of the Christian world has fallen into the same trap.

- God is love and He wants me to be happy.

- It is my right to be happy because God is love.

- It is my right to love and be loved.

- He/She loves God, loves me, and we are happy.

There are a number of people demanding that gay-identified Christians have a right to enjoy the tenderness and companionship of an intimate relationship. Yet the truth is that neither the gay nor the straight Christian has any rights at all, but *together* we are slaves of God and slaves to righteousness (Romans 6:18; 22). Life, liberty, and the pursuit of happiness should be subject to the boundaries created by God and not running parallel to His commands. Consequently, whether we are gay or straight, married or single, with or without children, we are together dependent on and recipients of God's gracious gifts.

And whether we understand why the Lord gives some things and withholds other blessings from us, we can be sure that He is good and withholds no good thing from those who love Him (Psalm 84:11).

These three areas – worries, riches, and pleasures – are taken seriously by Jesus in the parable of the sower and can seriously distract believers from greater maturation in their faith. Those three areas alone will challenge a Christian's ability to bring and keep their SSA under God's loving jurisdiction. May I encourage you to remain watchful over your patch of ground, always keeping an eye out for signs of regrowth? Those three weeds will gladly volunteer to overtake your spiritual garden again!

Determine other sources of distraction

What if you are up to date with your spiritual gardening and able to keep the troublesome trio of worries, riches, and pleasures well under control? In order to live contentedly in the life God has determined, it is good to remain vigilant toward other sources of distraction.

Some distractions are of our own making and are easy to eliminate. Many years ago I stopped having the newspaper delivered to my door. Seemingly incapable of reading it with any discrimination, I lost hours to newsprint, to the detriment of anything else. Realizing that I was spending more time reading about the ways of the world than the ways of God convinced me to take action and I stopped buying a newspaper.

Years later, of course, I have had to face the same battle with my phone and tablet! In an attempt to retain the supremacy of Scripture in my life, both devices are now turned off by mid-evening and banned from the bedroom. But, I have to confess, the fight goes on during daylight hours.

Some distractions are of our own making and are less easy to eliminate. Long after I had stopped participating in same-sex sexual behaviour I was still struggling with the whole area

214

of emotional enmeshment with other women. Some of the dependency issues were reciprocal and others were strictly one-sided. I have written about the subject of emotional dependency in both of my previous books and will not pursue that subject here except to say that any relationship that is not centred in Christ and causes us to relegate our relationship with Jesus into second or third place is a distraction that requires our intention and attention to correct. Four quick personal questions help keep any budding friendship in perspective:

- Do I think about this person more than I think about Jesus?
- Do I value the thoughts and ideas of this person more than I rate the teachings of Christ and God's Word?
- Do I want to please this person more than I want to please Christ?
- Is my sense of well-being and happiness dependent on this person's view of me, or on who Jesus says I am?

Having been enmeshed in relationships that are unhealthy at best and downright idolatrous at worst, I know how hard it is to disentangle oneself from the painful dilemma of emotional dependency. Like rampant bindweed, these dependent relationships squeeze the life out of any godly plant that is trying to mature in Christ. We can bring that relationship to an end, but snapping off the seen weed is not enough and help is required to source and address the root system that is feeding this proliferation of growth. Only systematic sourcing and digging out of the roots on a regular basis with the help of others will ever protect the godly plants and give opportunity for fruitfulness.

The distraction of responsibility: The elder son

The Manchester United and Northern Ireland soccer player, George Best, was as famous for his off-field partying as he was for his soccer skills on the pitch. One of his best-remembered quips was: "I spent 90% of my money on women, drink and fast cars. The rest I wasted." It is a sentiment that could have easily come from the lips of the prodigal son whose story we read in Luke 15. Unlike poor George, this young man came to his senses and returned home, determined to seek his father's forgiveness and take on the position of servant. The aged father, however, is so delighted at the return of his once-lost son that, instead of chastising the boy, he throws open his house and hosts a party to end all parties.

While the younger son was following a hedonistic lifestyle, the elder son had done the right thing and had remained dutiful, responsible, obedient, hardworking, and disciplined. He had watched his father mourn the loss of his good-for-nothing son and now, after completing yet another long day in the field, the elder son returns home to find a party in full swing. Had nobody even thought to send him a message?

This party, however, did not consist of a hurriedly bought six-pack and a bag of peanuts from the local shop. By the time the elder brother got back to the house, the food had been prepared and was cooked, musicians had been found and were playing, and guests had been invited and were dancing. We read that the elder son only got to know of this celebration because as he approached the house, he heard the music and dancing (verse 25). All of this effort and cost simply because his wasteful younger brother bothered to come home. Is it any wonder the elder of the two sons would not go into the house and join in the merriment?

216

So his father came outside and called him. Then he burst out, "Look, how many years have I slaved for you and never disobeyed a single order of yours, and yet you have never given me so much as a young goat, so that I could give my friends a dinner? But when that son of yours arrives, who has spent all your money on prostitutes, for him you kill the calf we've fattened!"

Luke 15:28b–30, J. B. PHILLIPS

This short paragraph says everything about the relationship between the father and his son. Beginning a sentence with the word "Look" is pretty confrontational and when, despite being the son and heir, the elder son refers to his work as slaving for years we realize this conversation isn't going to end well. Did he see himself as a son, or a faithful and obedient employee? As he continues his tirade against his father, we witness the result of years of pent-up hurt, frustration, and anger being vomited out in that one short scene.

The distraction of responsibility: Martha

As Jesus and his disciples were on their way, he came to a village where a woman named Martha opened her home to him.She had a sister called Mary, who sat at the Lord's feet listening to what he said. But Martha was distracted by all the preparations that had to be made. She came to him and asked, "Lord, don't you care that my sister has left me to do the work by myself? Tell her to help me!"

"Martha, Martha," the Lord answered, "you are worried and upset about many things, but few things are needed – or indeed only one. Mary has chosen what is better, and it will not be taken away from her."

Luke 10:38–42

217

We looked in some detail at Jesus' relationship with these siblings back in chapter 10. It was clear that He not only enjoyed time with them, but that they really possessed a good understanding of His purpose and mission.

Although people certainly went to the synagogue and Temple to worship, Jewish belief held that the home was the centre of religious activity. It was there that one was taught and learned to worship God. Part of a Jew's religious duty was to provide hospitality to all, but especially to any visiting rabbis. Martha was the eldest woman in the house and, as such, was fulfilling her responsibilities as a Jewish woman. But in fulfilling societal expectations, Martha was missing out on the main event. And we see that accomplishing what was "good" distracted Martha from receiving what was "best": intimacy with her Lord.

Her emotional outburst, "Lord, don't you care that my sister has left me to do the work by myself? Tell her to help me!" indicates that Martha knew she was missing out on something better, but her sense of duty and the expectations of others prevented her from listening first-hand to Jesus. Not only did this result in a flash of exasperation toward her sister and her teacher, Martha's failure to absorb the more subtle truth of Christ probably helped facilitate her response to Jesus at the death of her brother, Lazarus.

The outburst of the elder sister and the lengthier diatribe of the elder son show me that they had allowed their responsibilities to displace their relationship with Jesus in the first instance and with the father in the second. Martha had forgotten to prioritize her life and the elder son had forgotten who he was in relation to his father. Both were distracted, but how could they get back on the right track?

The importance of focus

Too many men and women begin their Christian journey as people who walk with Jesus but end up disillusioned or burnt out because they unwittingly morph from walking with Jesus into working for Jesus. This state isn't only applicable to those who are employed by Christian organizations or agencies on a full-time basis, but is also a real danger for all believers. After the elder brother's rant, the father responds: "My son... you are always with me, and everything I have is yours" (Luke 15:31). In this one sentence the father makes three critical points:

- **Identity: "My son".** The older brother may have been operating with the mindset of a servant, but the father states the man's true identity as his son.

- **Position: "You are always with me".** Just because the son spent all of his time with the servants working in the field, the man's actual home was in the big house with his father. If he had remained close to his father relationally and not just physically, then the events around the youngest son's return would have been very different.

- **Wealth: "Everything I have is yours."** What was one fatted calf compared to the extravagances that were to hand on a daily basis for the son and heir?

The son in this story either never knew or had forgotten who he was, whose company he could be in, and the rich inheritance he had been given. It is possible that you or someone you know is living like the elder brother in this story. Diligence and application are fine qualities, but must come from a sound understanding of who we are, where we sit (Ephesians 2:6), and all the blessings that are available in Christ.

One of the meanings of the Hebrew word *yada* is to "know by experience". The older son needed to lay down his work tools for a while, come in from the field, and make himself at home in the father's house. Head knowledge of who he was and what he had available to him served no purpose when confronted with experiences that evoked an emotional response. This man had to return to his father in the big house and *yada* – know by experience – the truth.

Martha was in the same building as Jesus, but was not necessarily in earshot of what He was saying. Her service, as good as it was, was actually preventing her from knowing Him better. Jesus' words in Matthew 11 could have been spoken directly to this dear lady:

> Come to me, all you who are weary and burdened, and I will give you rest. Take my yoke upon you and learn from me, for I am gentle and humble in heart, and you will find rest for your souls. For my yoke is easy and my burden is light.

> Matthew 11:28–30, J. B. PHILLIPS

Addressing subjects such as attachment and loss, gender and sexual identity, past abusive situations and the like can be very tiring and time consuming. It is right to look at these areas, whether that is within the realm of professional counselling or through Christian programmes such as Living Waters,[60] but it is critical that our daily living emanates from the position adopted by Mary, sitting at the feet of Christ.

60   Living Waters' home page states: "Living Waters is a 20 week closed group for men and women seeking healing in their lives. It is an intensive and unique small group. Ultimately, we learn how to press into Jesus more deeply, allowing Him to meet our needs and transform us for His Kingdom purposes. With groups all over the world, and with over thirty years of ministering God's healing love, the Living Waters program is a proven path of healing." See http://desertstream.org/living-waters.

Such an over-focus on change in our "situation" and "issues" can lead us into loss of focus on the One who controls all outside situations and changes us on the inside. For instance, Elijah stood in the face of tremendous evil and demonstrated God's Lordship over all things as he performed amazing miracles. But even he grew tired, fell into despair, and lost his perspective on the overall situation (1 Kings 19:10). After feeding him and letting him sleep, God sent Elijah to Mount Horeb.

> The Lord said, "Go out and stand on the mountain in the presence of the Lord, for the Lord is about to pass by." Then a great and powerful wind tore the mountains apart and shattered the rocks before the Lord, but the Lord was not in the wind. After the wind there was an earthquake, but the Lord was not in the earthquake. After the earthquake came a fire, but the Lord was not in the fire. And after the fire came a gentle whisper. When Elijah heard it, he pulled his cloak over his face and went out and stood at the mouth of the cave. Then a voice said to him, "What are you doing here, Elijah?"
>
> 1 Kings 19:11–13

Elijah had to draw close to the gentle whisper in order to hear and receive from God, who subsequently corrected this prophet's incorrect assumption that he was the only prophet left. Then He continued to give Elijah further directions.

Early on in this chapter, we read Jesus' warning in Luke 8 about the dangers of "life's worries, riches and pleasures" that can prevent a believer from maturing in their faith. But Jesus doesn't leave this subject on a negative note, and in the following verse He says:

But the seed on good soil stands for those with a noble and good heart, who hear the word, retain it, and by persevering produce a crop.

Luke 8:15

In the next chapter we shall look at the necessity of perseverance, which is an antidote to distraction.

Section 5

The "land" we have been allocated may not be what we had hoped for, but it is still our inheritance. If it is flat and fertile, then we plant crops. And if it is rugged and hilly, we shepherd sheep. It is what we make it.

Chapter 13

Perseverance is a Sign of Maturity

> In any big household there are naturally not
> only gold and silver vessels but wooden and
> earthenware ones as well. Some are used for the
> highest purposes and some for the lowest. If a man
> keeps himself clean from the contaminations of evil
> he will be a vessel used for honourable purposes,
> clean and serviceable for the use of the master
> of the household, all ready, in fact, for any good
> purpose.
>
> 2 Timothy 2:20–21, J. B. PHILLIPS

In my thirty-year walk with the Lord, I have come to believe that temptations are intended to wear us down and destroy our relationship with God, whereas trials are intended to purify, strengthen, and bring us closer to God. Learning to differentiate between the two is critical if we are to respond correctly in each situation.

For instance, I did not find the first couple of years as a Christian easy. I had walked away from a relationship that I had invested in and intended to make permanent, and had relocated away from the gay society in which I moved. No one in my new Christian life knew anything about my past and so I dealt with, or not as the case may be, the enormous loss I experienced alone. At times, the temptation to drive to the city was enormous. It wasn't that I wanted to go there and sin, I just wanted to walk the familiar streets and feel as though I belonged. I did not return to that city for twenty-five years.

Trials, on the other hand, are initiated by God and that is why James exhorts us to count them all joy (James 1:2–3). In one of his farewell speeches Moses tells the Jews:

> Remember how the Lord your God led you all the way in the wilderness these forty years, to humble and test you in order to know what was in your heart, whether or not you would keep his commands.
>
> **Deuteronomy 8:2**

God-inspired trials are the heat that causes the dross, such as pride and self-seeking, in our hearts to surface. That dross is then skimmed off the surface and discarded. Every time this happens we become more Christ-like and more able to be a "vessel used for honourable purposes, clean and serviceable for the use of the master of the household, all ready, in fact, for any good purpose" (2 Timothy 2:22)

Knowing when to "flee from" and knowing when to "abide under" is vital if our same-sex attractions are to be brought under and remain under the Lordship of Christ. Scriptural direction for sexual temptation is clear and we are told, without exception, to flee from such enticement. Unfortunately, Samson chose to indulge.

Dan's man

In chapter 6 we looked at one of the twelve tribes of Israel – Dan – and how the people were disappointed with the allocation of land that God had given them. Dissatisfied with God's provision, the tribe failed to take possession of their inheritance. Many chose to relocate elsewhere in order to live a life that best suited them. This failure to obey God's direction soon resulted in an amalgamation of idol worship and true worship. This heralded the eventual fall of Israel away from the things of God. Those that remained in their inherited land fared little better and soon took local pagan women as wives, resulting, ultimately, in the extinction of the tribe.

Samson was the most famous member of this Danite clan. Set apart as a Nazirite[61] by God before birth, Samson was born to godly parents during the time when their tribal area was under Philistine rule. The Philistines were, without doubt, formidable opposition. Originating from Greece, these people had used iron not only to make weapons, but also to build chariots that were best suited to the flat land that lay between the foothills and the coast – God's gift to Dan. In Dan's favour, however, was the size of their tribe, some 60,000 odd, and they had previously proved themselves in warfare. Not only that, but they were also surrounded by a number of other tribes who, combined with the tribes east of the Jordan, were obligated, according to Deuteronomy 3:18–20, to help their fellow Israelites conquer the land (see Fig. 2) The greatest "weapon" the Danites had in their favour was God.

---

61   A full description of what was required of a Nazirite can be found in Numbers 6:1–21. In Hebrew the word *nazir*, simply means "to be separated or consecrated", and a man or woman could voluntarily take a Nazirite vow for a period of time, often lasting only thirty days, for any number of reasons. Although it was essentially a voluntary act chosen by an individual, it is worth noting that Samson's parents chose this commitment for their son for life. Two other individuals had this commitment chosen for them: the prophet Samuel (1 Samuel 2:8–28) and John the Baptist (Luke 1:13–17).

Fig. 2

God had given them the land, He had told them to conquer it and, historically, His speciality was in leading the weak and the dispossessed to victory! The Philistines had already dominated the Danites for twenty years before Samson's birth (see Fig. 3), but God clearly had in mind to rectify this situation by raising him up as another judge.

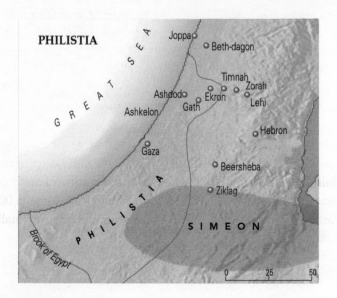

Fig. 3

Although Samson knew who he was and what he was meant to do, chapters 13 to 16 in the book of Judges reveal a sorry tale of a man who misused his God-given gifts and served his own purpose, rather than a man who fulfilled God's call on his life. The first recorded encounter we have of him with his parents rather sums up the man.

> Samson went down to Timnah and saw there a young Philistine woman. When he returned, he said to his father and mother, "I have seen a Philistine woman in Timnah; now get her for me as my wife." His father and mother replied, "Isn't there an acceptable woman among your relatives or among all our people? Must you go to the uncircumcised Philistines to get a wife?" But Samson said to his father, "Get her for me. She's the right one for me."
>
> **Judges 14:1–3**

As a young man, he dishonoured his parents, fraternized with the enemy, and slept with and married pagan women. When Samson didn't get his own way, he would use his strength to destroy those who double-crossed him, and in all of his relationships Samson failed to exhibit the fear of the Lord. For twenty years this judge failed to obey God's leading. Finally, when Samson was blinded, in chains, and subject to the humiliation of the enemy, he asked the Lord for the strength to obey. His hands were placed on the strategic pillars of the Philistine temple and his supernatural strength caused the stones to collapse. This killed him, along with some 3,000 feasting men and women. Only in his death did Samson finally begin to live a life pleasing to God.

The right one for me

The King James Bible translates Judges 14:3 as "she pleaseth me well", and isn't self-seeking pleasure at the core of all sin? However we may want to dress it up, we sin when we choose our desire over God's intention. Despite being stirred by God's Holy Spirit (Judges 13:25), careful reading of chapter 14 illustrates in what little esteem Samson held such a gift.

As we see from the map (Fig. 2), Timnah (highlighted in red) was located right on the border of the Philistine territory. This clearly shows that Samson chose to fraternize with the very people God had told him to conquer. Not only that, but he also chose to walk among their vines, despite knowing that he was forbidden to eat even one little grape. Clearly, in keeping with his rebellious nature, this man liked to walk on life's tightrope and it was therefore only a question of time before he fell. In Judges 14:6 we read that he broke the third Nazirite vow by touching the carcass of a lion he had killed – an action that led to problems later on. Samson's life shows that we can stubbornly pursue a life of self-gratification, or we can flip the coin and tenaciously live obediently within God's wishes.

Where are you right now? Are you fully ensconced in the "land" God has given you? Or are you border-hopping with the world, flirting with a lifestyle that excites your senses but will ultimately move you away from God's plan for your life? Are you walking through the enemy's vineyard, thinking that you are strong enough to resist the lure of just one measly grape? Or have you gone further and already engaged in something secret (Samson's parents were unaware of the lion incident), continually returning to eat the sweet honey, forgetting that it is taken from the centre of something that is dead and rancid?

It is not too late

Unfortunately, Samson didn't come to his senses until he had been blinded and imprisoned as a slave by the Philistines. In between bouts of hard labour, he was brought out to entertain the enemy who jeered and humiliated this man of God. Samson's life was, for the most part, a life of disobedience and failure. And yet, in Hebrews 11, he is listed with other men and women of faith.

> And what more shall I say? I do not have time to tell about Gideon, Barak, Samson and Jephthah, about David, Samuel and the prophets, who through faith conquered kingdoms, administered justice, and gained what was promised; who shut the mouths of lions,quenched the fury of the flames, and escaped the edge of the sword; whose weakness was turned to strength; and who became powerful in battle and routed foreign armies.
>
> **Hebrews 11:32–34**

Samson was a man of faith but, unlike others on the list, he did not live faithfully in his calling until right at the very end when he finally realized that all he possessed came from God. In his weak position as a chained and blinded slave, God's man finally lived up to his calling. Relying on another to position his hands on the pillar, this once self-reliant man called on the name of the Lord, resulting in victory for God's people. If we are wise, we can learn from this man without following in his footsteps.

The sin that so easily entangles

Have you ever stood on your own shoelace and ended up flat on your face? After a few years of faithful Christian living, regular believers will have done much to address the obvious sin areas in their life and can spot, with certain clarity, a direct attack on their person and faith. And it is at that point that Christians can be most vulnerable, because something as small as a spiritual shoelace can flaw the most committed of believers. In the Bible, only Jesus Christ has more names than Satan and, just as the names of Jesus describe His character, it is worth being reminded of some of Satan's characteristics:

- the accuser (Revelation 12:10)
- the angel of light (2 Corinthians 11:14)
- the deceiver (Revelation 12:9, NRSV)
- the enemy (Matthew 13:39)
- the father of lies (John 8:44)
- the god of this age (2 Corinthians 4:4)
- the man of lawlessness (2 Thessalonians 2:3)
- the man of sin (2 Thessalonians 2:3–4)
- a murderer (John 8:44)
- the power of darkness (Colossians 1:13–14, NKJ)

- the ruler of the kingdom of the air (Ephesians 2:2)
- a roaring lion (1 Peter 5:8)
- the prince of demons (Luke 11:15)
- the ruler of this world (John 12:31–32)
- the tempter (Matthew 4:3)
- the thief (John 10:10)
- the evil one (Ephesians 6:16)

Even this incomplete list reveals an enemy with whom we flirt at our peril. Is it any wonder that Proverbs 6:27 asks rhetorically, "Can a man scoop fire into his lap without his clothes being burned?"? After reading the encouraging list of men and women, many of whom remained faithful despite horrendous torture and death, the writer of Hebrews challenges his reader:

> Therefore then, since we are surrounded by so great a cloud of witnesses [who have borne testimony to the Truth], let us strip off and throw aside every encumbrance (unnecessary weight) and that sin which so readily (deftly and cleverly) clings to and entangles us, and let us run with patient endurance and steady and active persistence the appointed course of the race that is set before us...

> **Hebrews 12:1**, AMP

I love the phrase "readily (deftly and cleverly) clings to and entangles us". It conjures up every imaginable, underhanded scheme that Satan may deploy in his attempt to keep us from living a life pleasing to God.

A negative response

A number of years ago, long before the time of digital cameras, a friend of mine felt that it was right to destroy all the photographs of her previous girlfriends that she had in her possession. Explaining that looking at them just kept feeding that desire to return to an active gay life, Kay (not her real name) decided to burn her bridges, so to speak, and she put all of the photographs in the incinerator in the back garden, along with some books and magazines that she had previously held on to. Then she ceremoniously doused the pile with petrol and set it alight.

A few years later, after she had spent time skirting around the edges of the local lesbian community, Kay decided that she was tired of "trying to go straight", and gradually eased herself back into her old ways. She finally left town and started afresh with her new partner in another part of the country. Some years later I had opportunity to speak with Kay, and in the course of the conversation she brought up the incineration of her photographs and books. With hearty amusement, Kay told me that although she had destroyed the photographs that day, she had actually kept a box full of the negatives under her bed – just in case she ever changed her mind. We must never think that we are beyond being a victim of our own deceitful ways.

Running your race

As a school teacher, the summer term meant that I taught swimming in the outdoor pool, tennis, cricket, and athletics. Although I had a number of good athletes throughout the school who specialized in various athletic disciplines such as the 100 metres, long jump, and the 1,500 metres middle distance, all of them stayed together for the initial warm-up period. That session usually began with a gentle jog around the 400-metre track.

One girl, Nicola (not her real name), suffered badly from asthma and had to carry her inhaler at all times. She not only suffered from asthma but also had the least amount of stamina I have ever encountered in a student. Nicola was incapable of completing one full circuit and her droopy countenance and slow saunter over the final 150 metres of the warm up was painful to watch. However, once Nicola put on her spikes and approached the starting line of the 100-metre race this girl transformed into someone else: she was focused, determined, and fast. Many athletes are capable of running both the 100- and 200-metre races, but not Nicola, who could only run the one shorter distance. She knew what she was capable of and did it to the best of her ability. Nicola went on to break all of the school records in each age group at this distance.

What is your optimum race? You may know people who have left a life of active homosexuality and have, seemingly without too much effort, walked on into marriage and family life. There may be others who have committed to Christ and, despite years of faithful living, seemed to have experienced little or no change in their orientation or attraction. Does that mean that one has succeeded and the other has failed? Or does it mean that God has called us to follow different paths as we both journey toward Him?

Nicola may have wanted to be a 400-metre champion hurdler, but she didn't have the build, the stamina, or the skill-set to achieve such a dream. Spending time on specific skills for that particular discipline would have been frustrating and, for her, a complete waste of time.

The writer of Hebrews makes it clear that we are to run the "race that is set before us", and not some other person's race. The Greek word used for "set before", *prokeimai*, is only used five times in the whole of the New Testament. Interestingly, the next time it is used is in the following sentence regarding Jesus, "for the joy set before [*prokeimai*] him he endured the cross" (Hebrews 12:2). Is it any wonder the writer tells us to "fix our eyes" on Him in verse 2 and "consider" Him in verse 3? In running our particular race, however different that may be from those around us, we are not being called to do anything that our Lord Jesus has not already done. In focusing beyond the finish line, the joy set before Him, Jesus was able to endure the cross. On what or whom is our point of focus?

Abiding

The actual technique of grafting a scion into rootstock illustrates well the need for a believer to be embedded into the person of Jesus in order to receive all that He has for life and well-being. In chapter 5 we considered the importance of abiding in Christ so that we would mature in and bear fruit for God's Kingdom. "Abiding in" Christ is critical if we are to "abide under" the trials that will come our way, according to the apostle Paul as well as the writer of Hebrews. As a non-Greek scholar I thoroughly recommend W. E. Vine's *The Expanded Vine's Expository Dictionary of New Testament Words*[62] as an aid to a richer understanding of the Scriptures. According to Vine, this Greek word, *hypomonē*, is used elsewhere in Scripture to exhort the Christian to "abide under":

- trials generally (Luke 21:19)

- trials resulting from Christian service (2 Corinthians 6:4)

- trials prompted by God for the purpose of discipline (Hebrews 12:7)

- even when the trials are undeserved (1 Peter 2:20)

---

62   W. E. Vine, *The Expanded Vine's Expository Dictionary of New Testament Words*, Bethany House, 1984.

- continuing good deeds (Romans 2:7, KJV: "patient continuance")
- when producing fruit (Luke 8:15).

However unpleasant the process is and/or undeserved the situation, when we "abide under" the suffering or trial, we learn so much about the character of God and, in turn, about our own character. We may not think we can cope with one more bit of bad news or another difficult day. Even so, if we resist fleeing from the presenting problem, we learn that God's grace *is* sufficient (2 Corinthians 12:9), His strength far outweighs our weaknesses, and His foolishness is more trustworthy than the wisdom of man (1 Corinthians 1:25).

Undoubtedly there will be times when we don't understand God's involvement (or His seeming lack of involvement) in any given situation. There will also be times when running away seems preferable to staying put. But it is at these times that abiding under the stressor results in personal growth. And like any other behaviour pattern, the more it is exercised, the more habitual the behaviour becomes.

Elite athletes

There is a world of difference between a fun-runner and an elite athlete. Fun-runners fit their exercise into their everyday life, whereas training is central to the athlete's day. Elite runners organize their eating and sleeping patterns to optimize their race performance, and will readily forgo social invitations or holidays if there is a chance they will interfere with the training schedule. A fun-runner is happy to take part whereas an elite athlete runs to win. A fun-runner will stop when it begins to hurt but an elite athlete will, if it's not damaging their body, train through the pain.

The apostle Paul understood these differences. He made several references to athletics in his letters. He writes to the Corinthians:

> You've all been to the stadium and seen the athletes' race. Everyone runs; one wins. Run to win. All good athletes train hard. They do it for a gold medal that tarnishes and fades. You're after one that's gold eternally.

> **1 Corinthians 9:24–25,** *The Message*

The point Paul is making is really no different from the Scripture quoted at the beginning of this chapter. The apostle wrote to Timothy, likening a believer to a household vessel. Some, he writes, will remain as multi-functional bowls or containers used by the servants, but others will be transformed into fine quality vessels ready for the master's personal use. Paul makes it clear that this transformation is not just a random act, but is the result of intentional cleansing and purging and remaining uncontaminated. Just as a fun-runner won't convert, simply through aspirational feelings, into even a good runner – never mind an elite one – so a believer won't mature into someone useful to our Lord merely by wishful thinking.

Focused perseverance

All young athletes dream of winning a gold medal. They see their heroes on the television, basking in the glory of their victorious moment, and take note of the numerous plaudits that are subsequently bequeathed on the champion for the next few months. In today's climate, lucrative sponsorship deals and book or TV contracts ensure that the successful sportsperson is made financially secure for life. They are feted and admired by royalty and politicians alike.

Every young athlete dreams of winning a gold medal, but not every youngster is prepared to make the sacrifices necessary to give them even a chance of success. Pounding the streets on cold winter mornings, turning down pizza, or saying "no" to teenage socials requires far more than some vague desire for success. Vision, commitment, and inner drive propels the teenager out of bed in the early morning and back into bed early at night, even though friends taunt and tease because of the choices they make.

Giving God permission to dismantle and rebuild us for the sake of the Kingdom can sometimes feel similar to an endless pre-dawn run in the depth of winter. Addressing such issues as shame or guilt, self-loathing or narcissism is not straightforward or pain-free. Talking about the abuse you have received or even meted out to others requires commitment from you and help and encouragement from others. But it is worth it. Some of the most godly men and women I know have been those who have brought their same-sex attractions before the Lord, submitting them and indeed themselves to His refining fire. They have emerged as gold and silver vessels and prove most useful to the Master, whether in their own immediate vicinity or out on the worldwide stage.

Bob's testimony

Revd Bob Ragan is a true man of God whom I have the privilege of calling my friend. He has been the director of Regeneration, Northern Virginia (NoVA) since 1993. He provides spiritual direction and healing prayer, and coordinates support groups in the Washington, DC, metropolitan area. Bob has ministered in Europe, South America, Asia, and across the US and is an ordained deacon in the Anglican Church. Bob has kindly allowed me to use some of his story and we take it up during his late teenage years.

Although I walked with the Lord throughout college, I was wrestling with my unwanted same-sex attractions. I didn't know who to talk to or how to process these feelings. After college, I walked away from the Lord. I began dating a man I worked with and entered into a six-year relationship with him. I thought I had found my Mr Right. When that relationship fell apart, I got involved in an emotionally destructive, codependent relationship which lasted for four years. From there, I descended into alcohol abuse and short-term encounters.

During those eleven years that I walked as a gay-identified man, the Lord never stopped pursuing me. In 1986, He placed Christians in my path which ended up with my rededication to the Lord in August of 1987. This time, however, I asked Jesus not only to be Savior but also Lord! I invited Him to be Lord over every aspect of my life, including my sexuality. In January of 1989, I found out about Regeneration Ministries and met with Alan Medinger. Here began my journey of becoming – becoming the man God created me to be.

Pursuing change

My early years of process were a time of restless activism. I read every Christian book I could find on the topic, went to every conference I could attend, and sought pastoral care. Although these were helpful things to do, I was the one in control of my process. I was focused on the healing of my soul rather than the Healer of my soul. I had not learned to yield my control up to the Lord.

My early childhood flesh pattern was to be a parent pleaser. This developed into my becoming a people pleaser and then a God pleaser. Every time the church doors were open, I was there. God intervened, revealing I was trying to manipulate Him to love me more, thereby cheapening the work of the Cross. God showed me there was nothing I could do to get Him to love me more than He already did. He also showed me nothing I did could stop Him from loving me. However, this wasn't "sloppy agapé", allowing for license. God loved me enough to accept me where I was, but loved me too much to leave me there. He is always at work, beckoning me to higher purpose and calling.

Pursuing Christ

I began to realize my process wasn't about the changing of behaviors but the changing of my heart. We become that on which we are focusing. Constantly focusing on changing my behaviors was focusing on myself. It was helpful to understand and see the impact of my past, but knowing "facts" was not going to result in freedom. I could know every cause for my sexual and relational brokenness, and these facts in and of themselves would not provide the freedom for which I was yearning. I needed something far deeper to happen in my heart.

I had a seventeen-year addiction to masturbation and pornography. My focus was on sobriety and a record. I allowed my "record" to be proof of my righteousness. Instead of resting in who I am in Christ, who is my righteousness, I rested in my behaviors, which always failed in the end. My victory began when I stopped keeping a record. My behavior changed when I began to invite Jesus, practicing His presence, in the midst of my struggles. As I allowed Him to enter into my struggles and pain, He taught me perseverance. Jesus bore the burden with me.

Whatever, Lord

Jesus has asked me the same two questions throughout my process and I believe will continue to do so until the day I am with Him. He asks me: Bob, will you follow Me no matter what the cost? Will you trust Me?

I also remember early in my process being asked more directly if I would follow Him even if I did not experience further release from my unwanted SSA. My commitment to Jesus cannot be based upon my expectations nor my definition of "healing". My commitment has to be based solely on my yielding to His Lordship without conditions. My deepest desire is to know and be known by God, and then also to know and be known by others. My deepest drive is for true intimacy, the kind God created me to know and experience. I've turned to many sources of false intimacy which only temporally gratified me but did not fulfill me. My walk has been one of endurance, learning the source of all my struggles. That which is driving me, is my heart yearning for fulfillment. It has taken more than twenty-five years to see that I looked to the finite, but was hungering for the infinite.

A surprising turn of events

As I entered more profoundly into relationship with my Beloved, being affirmed by my loving Father, my inner core was being changed. The more I stopped looking for causes and entered into greater intimacy with God, the more I became of the man God created me to be. My intimacy with God has impacted all of my relationships including those with women.

God did cause me to experience attractions to women. But I had fallen so in love with Him [that] in 2007 I knew He was calling me to embrace celibacy. How ironic that the change I initially had hoped for did happen, but God had something much deeper for my soul. Do I still experience loneliness in my state of singleness? Yes! But my Beloved is always there – not to remove it, but to walk me through it. My loneliness will be fully assuaged only on the day I see Him face to face.

Long-term prognosis

Since 1987, I have gone from struggle to perseverance. Jesus proved His faithfulness to me each time I allowed Him to walk me through my pain, loneliness, and challenges. I began to see with divine objectivity that everything which happens in my life is part of my process, and an opportunity for my becoming. He turns my failures into learning experiences. He reveals His compassion and love for me when I call on Him. His mercy always breaks my heart and draws me back to Him.

I am still in my process of becoming. I accept what is in the moment and look forward with holy anticipation to the not yet. I am my Beloved's and my Beloved is mine. Here I am finding the infinite my heart has been searching for these many years.

Divine determination

Bob walks in the footsteps of the saints of old. Hebrews 11 is often referred to as the "Believer's Hall of Fame", simply because real heroes and heroines of the faith are mentioned. Even today we read harrowing reports of men, women, and children in the Middle East, Far East, and parts of Africa still suffering and dying for their faith. The Amplified Bible describes Moses as follows:

[Motivated] by faith he left Egypt behind him, being
unawed and undismayed by the wrath of the king; for
he never flinched but held staunchly to his purpose
and endured steadfastly as one who gazed on Him Who
is invisible.

Hebrews 11:27

Without doubt, walking away from homosexual behaviour and living with a propensity toward same-sex attraction can be extremely hard at times, but it is not impossible. Taking the focus off self and off our *issues* and directing it onto Christ is the first step towards God's definition of wholeness. As we abide in Christ and fix our eyes upon Him, we can abide under and endure the necessary pruning and refining that is both ordained and carried out by our ever-loving and good God.

Chapter 14

Scarred but Steadfast

When peace, like a river, attendeth my way,
When sorrows like sea billows roll;
Whatever my lot, Thou has taught me to say,
It is well, it is well with my soul.[63]

It is well with my soul

Born in 1828, Horatio Spafford rose to fame as a successful lawyer in Chicago, USA. He married in 1861 and started a family soon after. Spafford became a partner in a law firm, a prominent member of a large Presbyterian church, and a friend and supporter of the great American evangelist Dwight L. Moody. Life was good.

However, the good life was not to last and in 1871, having invested most of his fortune in real estate, the family lost nearly everything when the city of Chicago was burned to the ground. Instead of mourning their personal loss, however, the Spaffords spent the following two years investing time and providing practical help to those who suffered most from the devastation.

In 1873, the couple and their four daughters decided to join the evangelist Dwight L. Moody on his crusade tour of the United Kingdom. Their aim was not only to be available to the evangelist, but also to enjoy a family holiday. Unfortunately, important business commitments forced the family to alter their plans. It was agreed that the wife and girls would sail to the UK as arranged, and Spafford would finish his work and catch a later ship.

63   Horatio G. Spafford, "It is Well With My Soul",1873.

All did not go to plan. Out in the Atlantic, the first sailing boat was struck by a steamer ship and sank. Although his wife was saved and taken on to Wales, the four girls aged between two and eleven years went down with the ship. It was nine days later when Horatio Spafford received a telegram from his wife saying, "Saved alone." He immediately took a sailing boat to join her in Wales.

On board that later ship, a mere two weeks after the tragedy, Spafford joined the captain on the bridge. "A careful reckoning has been made," said the captain, "and I believe we are now passing the place where the *de Havre* was wrecked. The water is three miles deep." On receiving this news, Horatio Spafford went down into his cabin, sat at his desk and wrote his famous hymn.

When peace, like a river, attendeth my way,
When sorrows like sea billows roll;
Whatever my lot, Thou has taught me to say,
It is well, it is well with my soul

Though Satan should buffet, though trials should come,
Let this blest assurance control,
That Christ has regarded my helpless estate,
And hath shed His own blood for my soul.

My sin, oh, the bliss of this glorious thought!
My sin, not in part but the whole,
Is nailed to the cross, and I bear it no more,
Praise the Lord, praise the Lord, O my soul!

And Lord, haste the day when my faith shall be sight,
The clouds be rolled back as a scroll;
The trump shall resound, and the Lord shall descend,
Even so, it is well with my soul.

It is well with my soul,
It is well with my soul,
It is well, it is well with my soul.

A strong foundation

How can a man who has seen most of his buisness investments wiped out by the great Chicago fire and then, only two years later, is told of the drowning of his four daughters at sea, write a hymn declaring the wellness of his soul? The prophet Jeremiah writes this:

> This is what the Lord says: "Let not the wise man boast of his wisdom or the strong man boast of his strength or the rich man boast of his riches, but let him who boasts boast about this: that he understands and knows me, that I am the Lord, who exercises kindness, justice and righteousness on earth, for in these I delight," declares the Lord.
>
> **Jeremiah 9:23–24**

If Spafford had put his trust in his vast riches and possessions, the man would have been found wanting after the great Chicago fire. Neither would his fine skills as a lawyer have helped him in his bereavement. It wasn't Spafford's self-reliance that enabled him to state that it was well with his soul; it was his deep relationship with Jesus. Through every trial and tragedy, Spafford held on to an unshakable faith in a good God who knows the end from the beginning. The rest of his life continued to be both tragic and eventful and yet, through all of the turbulence, both Spafford and his family remained faithful to the One who called them and fruitful in His service.[64]

64   For more information on this family and the incredible legacy that continues to this day please go to http://www.spaffordcenter.org/.

How big is your rock?

A number of years ago, I would speak at various conferences and retreats both in the UK and overseas. Sometimes I would receive a small personal gift from a delegate. It was on one such occasion in Turku, Finland, that a lady handed me a pack of her handmade greetings cards.

These cards were fun, cartoon-like pictures illustrating various aspects of our relationship with God. One in particular challenged me deeply. The card showed a little figure waving a small Finnish flag standing on what I thought was planet earth. But, on closer inspection, I realized that this little figure was actually standing on an enormous rock!

I realized that my own vision of God, my rock, was far removed from this depiction. As I studied the simple cartoon, the Holy Spirit showed me that instead of standing confident on something strong and immovable, I saw myself, in a Christian sense, balancing rather precariously on a pebble – hoping that I wouldn't fall off! Although I would have been able to reel off a number of descriptions of God as my "stronghold", "shield", and "defender", it was clear that I *operated* out of a less secure base.

What an eye-opener! Since that time, I have used this cartoon to assess my heart's understanding of the solidity of my relationship with my Heavenly Father. This has proved most useful in times of difficulty and stress. When tempted through anxiety or fear to shrink the ground on which I stand, I remind myself of this cartoon and the Scripture Psalm 62:1–2:

> Truly my soul finds rest in God; my salvation comes from him.
> Truly he is my rock and my salvation; he is my fortress, I shall never be shaken.

On what are you standing today: a rock or a pebble? Or is it possible, because of the struggles you are currently facing, that you don't even feel as though you are above ground?

Waiting...

> I waited patiently for the Lord; he turned to me and heard my cry. He lifted me out of the slimy pit, out of the mud and mire; he set my feet on a rock and gave me a firm place to stand. He put a new song in my mouth, a hymn of praise to our God. Many will see and fear and put their trust in the Lord.
>
> Psalm 40:1–3

In this world of speed-dialling, speed-dating, and speed-reading, the first line of Psalm 40, "I waited patiently for the Lord", seems incongruous. There was a time when I would marvel at the fact I could access a book in a foreign library without having to leave the comfort of my own house, but now I tut petulantly at the computer screen if connection takes longer than a nanosecond!

I recently received an email from a lady who was clearly frustrated with her current status. Explaining that she committed herself to Christ some twelve years ago, left her lesbian relationship ten years ago, and had now been celibate for eight years, the correspondent asked in desperate tones: "When will I change?" How long is a piece of string? Is there a piece of string?

I don't chastise her for being frustrated. Waiting is hard, but I have seen that it need not be purposeless or fruitless. I have kept a spiritual journal since January 1988. It began the first month I arrived at the Christian ministry Love in Action in San

Rafael, California. I have often used passages of it to remind myself of times when God has moved powerfully, and this brings great encouragement when I find myself in a new place of waiting. As I remind myself of God's past faithfulness, I can turn those remembrances into praise. These times of praise ease the discomfort of the current period and remind me that waiting on the Lord is not in vain.

Waiting... for the Lord

It is my hope that as you have been reading this book, you've seen same-sex attraction not as something "out there" almost running parallel to our Christian walk, but more as the context of ongoing opportunities to mature in our Christianity. How we interpret our current situation is dependent on making God's vision our vision. Starting in a comparable place to the psalmist, that of standing in a slimy pit of mud and mire, let us take a brief look at some of Psalm 40.

A time of waiting is what we make of it. It can be a time of wallowing in the quagmire of self-pity, bemoaning our fate, or – instead of waiting and wallowing – we may choose to transform the time of waiting into a time of doing. That is not, however, necessarily a good choice. In an attempt to escape our sorry predicament, we may try relentless scrambling up the cold, wet, and slime-ridden walls, looking for non-existent handholds and footholds. This can be both exhausting and demoralizing. A resulting sense of failure and increasing fatigue often produces feelings of depression. I have certainly partaken in both extremes of behaviour: self-pity and striving.

But there is a better way. The waiting in this psalm, and for us, is not without focus or purpose. This waiting is not a mere hiatus in time, but a period spent fixed on hearing from the Lord, sensing His presence, and/or seeing Him at work in specific situations. There is an "active passivity" in this kind of intentional waiting: we are not trying to fix circumstances or heal ourselves, but are focused on the One who, as my friend Bob Ragan put it, is the Healer of our soul.

He turned to me and heard my cry

To be heard: isn't that what we all want? During your time of trial or distress, a number of people may well pause, turn your way, and hear your cry for help. Some may turn on their heel, blocking their ears to your situation. Others may try hauling you out of the pit by attempting to convince you that homosexual behaviour is perfectly acceptable to God. And there will be those who seek to help you in a way that is fully in agreement with your understanding of Scripture.

However, no matter how willing, how accomplished, and how well-qualified our human assistants may be, our focus must always be on the Lord. We must learn from the psalmist David who waited patiently for the Lord. Counsellors, books, conferences, and various discipleship programmes can be a welcome *addition to* our waiting on the Lord, but they are never an adequate *substitution for* it.

Is that all?

Now, if all the Lord could offer were a listening ear, then His presence would be no more helpful than our dear friends or skilled counsellors. But God is active.

The Canaanite woman in Matthew 15 cried out to Jesus for the healing of her demon-possessed daughter. And Jesus, impressed by her great faith, granted the woman her request. Despite being rebuked by the crowd, two blind men sitting by the roadside cried out to Jesus for mercy. He stopped and asked them what they wanted Him to do. At their response, Jesus had compassion on them and touched their eyes. Immediately they received their sight and followed Him (Matthew 20:34).

Ten lepers stood at a distance from Jesus and called out to Him, asking for pity. As they obeyed His direction, every one of them was cleansed (Luke 17:14).

Jesus not only turns to us and hears our cry, but *He does something about it.* In the three examples I cited above, Jesus clearly chose to heal those afflicted. But we know from experience that God does not always respond in direct accordance with our various prayer requests. And it is no different when we petition Him over the several areas associated with same-sex attraction. However, we can be confident that if we wait on the Lord, He will act on our behalf and for our best. In Psalm 40, we read that God gives David a sense of stability and confidence.

> He lifted me out of the slimy pit, out of the mud and mire; he set my feet on a rock and gave me a firm place to stand.
>
> Psalm 40:2

God is relational and personal. It is God who raises us up, God who lifts us away from this place of discomfort. It is He who places us on a secure footing, thus ensuring we are in a position of His strength. God's lifting up does not guarantee a change in feelings, desires, or long-term outlook. But it does mean that God positions us in a stronger place from which we can then look at our situation. It is putting into practice what C. S. Lewis wrote about in his "Meditations in a Toolshed" that I mentioned earlier in chapter 10. We need to be positioned so that we line up with the sunbeam. Although we may still be "in the toolshed", our vision has altered immeasurably. Now we can see beyond the door, past the swaying trees and the sun, and right into God's very throne-room.

Are you, like the psalmist, currently standing in the spiritual equivalent of a pit? Are the four walls that imprison you and a far-off sky overhead all that you can see? Is it taking all your energy and focus just to keep your feet from slipping in knee-deep mud or a waist-high bog? I have certainly been in that place. But I can testify that when I stopped my fruitless struggling, fixed my gaze upward, and allowed God His rightful position as Lord of every aspect of my life, He responded by standing me in a spacious place. I was secure in my footing and clear in my vision of Him. My circumstances hadn't changed at all, but my relationship with the Lord had.

A major step in placing and keeping our same-sex attractions under the Lordship of Christ is to cultivate an attitude that is counter-culture to the attitude so prevalent in society today. Individualism and self-determination are but two characteristics of the developed world and are an antithesis to Christ's way of relinquishment. If anyone could claim a sense of personal entitlement, it was Jesus. But in Philippians 2:6, J. B. Phillips' version states that Jesus "stripped himself of all privilege[s and rightful dignity]". To recognize that we, like Christ, are not of this world (John 17:16) is critical if we are to walk His walk here on earth.

Knowing Christ

The major benefit of standing on a firm foundation and in a spacious place means that we are better positioned to know more of Christ. In chapter 5, I described some of the work that is required to grow good quality grapes. The choice of location for the vineyard, the quality of the rootstock, and the skill of the scion grafters all combine to give the intended grape harvest the best possible start.

Continued attention by the vinedresser through feeding, watering, and the support of the branches along the wire safeguards the burgeoning crop through mid-season. In a spiritual sense, this is our time of knowing Christ more intimately and receiving all that He has to offer. The apostle Paul writes:

> I want to know Christ – yes, to know the power of
> his resurrection and participation in his sufferings,
> becoming like him in his death, and so, somehow,
> attaining to the resurrection from the dead.
>
> **Philippians 3:10–11**

I will not even pretend to know the full meaning of these two verses or attempt to explain the enormity of Christ's suffering. But, within the context of same-sex attraction, I offer these thoughts.

Focus and priority

The first thing Paul mentions in Philippians 3:10 is that he wants to know Christ. This has nothing to do with doctrine, or the Lord's teaching, or the facts about His death and resurrection. Those are all extremely important, but are not what the apostle is saying in this verse. He wants to *gnonai* Jesus. While this Greek word is rightfully translated as "to perceive" or "to get to know", it is also a Jewish idiom for sexual intercourse between a man and a woman. That is how much Paul wanted to know his Saviour!

Paul wants the intimacy that is reserved for a husband and wife to be present in his relationship with Christ. He wants complete oneness: to be in Christ and for Christ to be in him. He never married and I am sure there were times when he felt keenly the absence of a spouse. However, the first part of Philippians 3:10 gives tremendous insight into this man of God. Paul had succumbed to a greater love than that which anyone or anything in this world could offer – the love of Jesus. Everything, even the companionship of a wife, paled in the presence of his Saviour and Lord. It is for this reason that Paul could write with such passion to his dear friends in Ephesus:

> For this reason I kneel before the Father, from whom every family in heaven and on earth derives its name. I pray that out of his glorious riches he may strengthen you with power through his Spirit in your inner being, so that Christ may dwell in your hearts through faith. And I pray that you, being rooted and established in love,may have power, together with all the Lord's holy people, to grasp how wide and long and high and deep is the love of Christ, and to know this love that surpasses knowledge – that you may be filled to the measure of all the fullness of God.

> Ephesians 3:14–19

Conviction – not good ideas – maintains our walk

At some point good ideas will become bad ideas. I know a number of Christian men and women who ceased to engage in homosexual behaviour because it was someone else's good idea. Second-hand conviction of sin is unsustainable when difficult choices have to be made.

I started to become interested in Christianity while teaching at a girls' boarding school in Australia. When off duty, the boarding staff would hang out with each other and chat. I remember talking to one of the Christian teachers, Anne, about my need to become a Christian. "I'm happy enough as I am," I told her. Anne thought for a moment and said, "Imagine a dog lying in the backyard gnawing on its favourite bone. It's happy enough with what it has, but what if the owner came to the back door with a large juicy steak? What dog wouldn't leave its favourite bone in order to get something better?"

Although it was a further six months and a 12,000-mile journey back to the UK before I chose to leave the familiar "bone" of homosexual behaviour in favour of the "juicy steak" of Christianity, I have never lost the impact of that simple analogy. In the early years of my faith there were many times when I wanted to return to that favourite bone in the yard. It was old and familiar and comfortable. After all, I tried to reason with myself, I had been happy enough with it at the time, so surely I could be happy enough with it again.

But I had tasted of the Lord and He was good (Psalm 34:8). And in His goodness, He had convicted me of the sin of homosexual behaviour. To return to the bone in the backyard was to reject Him and His plans for me. As I said very early on in this book, well-meaning believers must not jump in with Christian rules and deny the homosexual seeker or young believer the *right* to be convicted of their sinful behaviour. Conviction, repentance, and commitment are some of the building bricks a believer with same-sex attraction will need if they are to walk faithfully with Christ. Behaviour modification and people-pleasing are little more than sinking sand when the storms of life begin to blow: they cannot sustain a journey forward.

Pruning the vine, cleansing the Temple

Pruning the vine during the winter months in preparation for another cycle of growth is not too dissimilar to Jesus' cleansing of the Temple that we read about in the Gospels. God's people have always waxed and waned in their relationship with Him. At one point, not too long before He thrust them into exile in Babylon, God spoke through the prophet Jeremiah:

> But look, you are trusting in deceptive words that are worthless. "Will you steal and murder, commit adultery and perjury, burn incense to Baal and follow other gods you have not known, and then come and stand before me in this house, which bears my Name, and say, 'We are safe'– safe to do all these detestable things? Has this house, which bears my Name, become a den of robbers to you? But I have been watching! declares the Lord…"
>
> **Jeremiah 7:8–11**

Some 600 years later, Jesus, having just wrecked the Court of the Gentiles, stands and quotes first from Isaiah and then from Jeremiah:

> "It is written," he said to them, "'My house will be called a house of prayer,' [Isaiah 56:7] but you are making it 'a den of robbers' [Jeremiah 7:11]."
>
> **Matthew 21:13, inserts mine**

Both the exchange of money from regular currency into Temple currency and the purchasing of unblemished birds and animals for sacrifice were legitimate practices in the time of Christ. The problem that Jesus had was two-fold. The first was location. The money exchange and the purchasing of animals should have taken place in the grounds outside of the Temple but, over the years, boundaries had become blurred and the traders gradually encroached into the Temple proper. Secondly, although the occupations of money changer and animal seller were legitimate, the methods used were anything but. This is not the place to explore their actions further. Suffice it to say that there was much collusion between them and the Temple priests regarding the exchange rate and the quality control of home-reared animals for sacrifice.

Since childhood, Jesus had passed through this internal market scene many times without commenting or acting. It might have been tempting to conclude that His silence implied acceptance of their attitude and behaviour. But nothing could have been further from the truth. To see their disrespect and lack of understanding of the things of God must have touched Jesus deeply and, although these people were in the Lord's house on a daily basis, their actions revealed that their hearts were far from His. And then one day, without warning, Jesus acted and cleansed the Temple (albeit briefly on this occasion) declaring:

> "Look, your house is left to you desolate. For I tell you, you will not see me again until you say, 'Blessed is he who comes in the name of the Lord'."
>
> Matthew 23:38–39; Luke 13:35

We are God's temple

We know that we are God's living temple, indwelt by His Holy Spirit. Paul tells the Corinthians:

257

> Do you not know that your bodies are temples of the
> Holy Spirit, who is in you, whom you have received from
> God? You are not your own; you were bought at a price.
> Therefore honour God with your bodies.
>
> **1 Corinthians 6:19–20**

We must not presume that the Lord's silence over certain thoughts or attitudes we harbour or behaviours in which we engage indicates His approval. In His good time, the Lord Jesus will point out elements of our lives that do not reflect the things of God. Our cooperation ensures that no matter how hard or lengthy the transformation process may be, He will be encouraging and strengthening us every step of the way. However, refusal to cooperate in His "renovation work" does not go unnoticed. Remember what was written in the book of Jeremiah?

> But look, you are trusting in deceptive words that are
> worthless. "Will you steal and murder, commit adultery
> and perjury, burn incense to Baal and follow other gods
> you have not known, and then come and stand before
> me in this house, which bears my Name, and say, 'We
> are safe'– safe to do all these detestable things? Has this
> house, which bears my Name, become a den of robbers
> to you? But I have been watching! declares the Lord…"
>
> **Jeremiah 7:8–11**

The Bible reminds us on several occasions that the "fear of the Lord is the beginning of wisdom". Wise believers regularly ask the Lord what King David asked so many years ago:

> Search me, God, and know my heart; test me and know
> my anxious thoughts. See if there is any offensive way in
> me, and lead me in the way everlasting.
>
> **Psalm 139:23–24**

We are loved too much to be left with vestiges of sin in this temple of ours. If we choose to stand in the framework of truth, lining up with who God says He is and living according to His wishes for our life, the blessings we receive are incalculable. Every time we choose His way over our way we get a clearer vision and understanding of God. Living in the outer courts of compromise is ultimately unsatisfactory. While attending to thoughts and engaging in behaviour that may be acceptable to current society, we are sabotaging our efforts to enter the rest found in the inner courts and the intimacy reserved only for the Holy of Holies.

Amy Carmichael

Amy Carmichael was born in Northern Ireland in 1867 and died in 1951 at the age of eighty-three. She had worked with marginalized women in the factory towns in northern England and, after a brief spell of missionary work in Japan, Carmichael took herself off to the southern tip of India to work among the Tamil people.

She founded the Dohnavur Fellowship in 1901, which sought out and rescued young girls, and eventually boys too, from temple prostitution. Carmichael was one of a kind. Her stubborn attitude and ceaseless activity often placed her in opposition to other, more genteel, missionaries in that area. In removing the children from temple prostitution, Carmichael also incurred the wrath of the Hindu priests. On a number of occasions she was taken to court on charges of being a kidnapper!

However, with the help of a few other determined and visionary Christians, this human dynamo also set up and ran hospitals, schools, and printing presses. A pioneer of modern anti-trafficking ministries and movements, she was determined not only to take children away from prostitution, but to create ways in which they could earn an income through skilled labour.

In 1931 she prayed, "God, please do with me whatever You want. Do anything that will help me to serve You better." That same day, Amy Carmichael had a fall and suffered fractures that would leave her essentially bedridden for the next twenty years until her death. Undeterred, the missionary ran the various ministries from her bed. Not only that, but she became a prodigious writer and, to prove the authenticity of her deep faith and resolve, a number of her books are still in print today some sixty odd years after her death.

Carmichael was no pushover. One illustration of her attitude can be found in a well-known response to a written question from an Edwardian lady back in London. "What is missionary life like?" wrote the enquirer. Amy wrote back a rather terse response simply stating, "Missionary life is simply a chance to die."

A chance to die – and trinkets or treasure

How do you view your life right now? Your attitude towards your current situation is critical in your call to mission, whether you are addressing issues connected to same-sex attraction, or have a loved one engaged in homosexual behaviour, or are walking alongside people who are in need of a confidante or encourager.

And we are all missionaries. Our lives reflect God's presence and power and purpose to a dark and needy world, irrespective of our location. Whether we live in a large city like Melbourne, Miami, or Manchester – or in some outpost in southern India – our call as believers is essentially the same. The apostle Paul writes:

> I eagerly expect and hope that I will in no way be
> ashamed, but will have sufficient courage so that now
> as always Christ will be exalted in my body, whether by
> life or by death. For to me, to live is Christ and to die is
> gain. If I am to go on living in the body, this will mean
> fruitful labour for me.
>
> **Philippians 1:20–22**

Christians with same-sex attraction issues stand alongside other Christians who also have to submit their thoughts, attitudes, and behaviours to the One who has created them and called them to obedience. Together we can encourage steadfastness in one another and urge our brothers and sisters in temple building.

> But I do concentrate on this: I leave the past behind
> and with hands outstretched to whatever lies ahead I go
> straight for the goal – my reward the honour of my high
> calling by God in Christ Jesus.
>
> **Philippians 3:13b–14**, J. B. PHILLIPS

A pilgrim path, by its very nature, is not an easygoing, six-lane highway. At the beginning of this chapter we read a little of Horatio Spafford's life story. He knew what it was to be well educated, productive, and wealthy. But he did not rely on earthly riches to determine his identity and character. In his mind, those things were mere trinkets compared to the treasure he had found in Christ. That being the case, when Spafford suffered monumental loss and bereavement, he was able to call on his spiritual investment to sustain and strengthen him through the darkest of personal circumstances.

Amy Carmichael worked ceaselessly for the betterment of Indian children in the late eighteenth and early nineteenth century. This was long before there was any structured organization financing to resource her vision. The unfortunate accident that left her bedridden for twenty years ensured that this energetic go-getting woman had to learn the reality of relinquishment and the capacity to be content in all situations. And yet it was in this difficult God-allowed crucible that Amy Carmichael found intimacy with Christ. And we are recipients of that legacy today.

In the poem that follows, Carmichael asks, with her customary directness, why every believer doesn't also carry the scars that Jesus bore.

Hast Thou No Scar?

Hast thou no scar?
No hidden scar on foot, or side, or hand?
I hear thee sung as mighty in the land,
I hear them hail thy bright ascendant star,
Hast thou no scar?

Hast thou no wound?
Yet, I was wounded by the archers, spent.
Leaned Me against the tree to die, and rent
By ravening beasts that compassed Me, I swooned:
Hast thou no wound?

No wound? No scar?
Yet as the Master shall the servant be,
And pierced are the feet that follow Me;
But thine are whole. Can he have followed far
Who has no wound nor scar?

Chapter 15

At Peace in the Land of Promise

> *Let Christ himself be your example as to what your
> attitude should be. For he, who had always been
> God by nature, did not cling to his prerogatives as
> God's equal, but stripped himself of all privilege
> by consenting to be a slave by nature and being
> born as mortal man. And, having become man, he
> humbled himself by living a life of utter obedience,
> even to the extent of dying, and the death he died
> was the death of a common criminal.*
>
> Philippians 2:5–8, J. B. PHILLIPS

Is it possible to live at peace in the land of promise?

In chapter 6 we looked at the tribe of Dan. They were
privileged people whom God had released from slavery
in Egypt. He had provided food and shelter and guidance
throughout their forty-year journey in and through the
wilderness. During that time, the Danites had grown in number
and were second only in size to the tribe of Judah. They, along
with all the other chosen peoples crossed the River Jordan
and began to make the Promised Land their own. And after
seven years of fighting, Joshua divided the land in accordance
with God's wishes. Dan was the last of the tribes to receive its
allocation and, although vast in number, it was actually given
the smallest land mass of all (Joshua 19:40–48).

But small does not mean bad. It was rich in natural resources
and had the security of shared borders with three other tribes.
Although we know that they struggled to take hold of what they
had been given, we read in 1 Chronicles 12:35 that they were

still able to muster 28,600 fighting men. These men joined with combatants from other tribes and met with David at Mount Hebron, determined to make him king. During the early part of David's reign, Azarel son of Jeroham was named as the tribe's leader (1 Chronicles 27:22). But that is the last mention of Dan as one of the chosen tribes. From that point on it is only recognized as the most northerly city in the country. What happened?

What I find most sobering of all is that Dan is not mentioned with all the other tribes in Revelation 7:5–7. In the vision recounted by John, this tribe fails to receive the seal of protection that ensures safeguard from the coming wrath of God. What can we learn from these people, and how can we apply that to our own lives?

Entitlement

Although it isn't stated in the Bible, it must have been irksome to be left until last on the allocation list and then, despite their being the biggest, to be given the smallest parcel of land. Had God forgotten their forty-year trudge through the wilderness? Didn't He notice how hard they had fought so that other tribes could receive their blessing? Didn't God realize what they really needed? Surely they deserved more for their faithful obedience?

What do you think you deserve? Do you look at the temptations you have overcome and the struggles and issues you have doggedly worked through and wonder if it has all been worth it? Where is the promised milk and honey?

It can be very tempting to think like the world and believe that effort should bring its just reward. I know that I was guilty of comparing my Christian journey with that of other people. During those early years of addressing my same-sex attraction, I would mentally line myself up against other women in the church and conclude that, when it came to blessings, I had been dealt a poor hand! This incorrect thinking served as ammunition for Satan, promoting self-pity and frustration. If left unchecked, thoughts snowball and lead us further away from God's defined path.

The following analogy and comments are sweeping generalizations to be held lightly. No analogy is fully accurate, let alone an infallible statement. But, I hope, this one will serve as a helpful starting point to stimulate you in further thinking.

Creating your own blessing

A portion of the Danites were dissatisfied with their ration and chose to move north. They found a place that was similar to their God-given land but without the problematic Philistines. Although their intentions were to follow God wholeheartedly, the Bible traces their slide into idolatrous ways and, under King Jeroboam, they even built a worship centre in the city – complete with a golden calf (1 Kings 12:28–30).

In what ways can this situation be likened to those Christian men and women who choose to "relocate" – remove the tension that occurs on the path of obedience – and regard homosexual behaviour and relationships as part of their overall Christian practice?

In what ways have you been or are you guilty of similar thinking and/or behaviour in regard to other sinful desires and patterns?

Heading for the hills

Another Danite group that stayed behind fared little better. They chose not to take hold of God's promises and utilize the natural resources in both land and sea. Fearful of the challenges that lay ahead, the people crowded into the foothills and eked out a meagre existence.

We can adapt a well-known phrase and create something applicable: "You can take the Hebrew out of Egypt, but you can't take Egypt out of the Hebrew." I think this idiom aptly describes this hill-hugging group of people. God did not intend His people to think like slaves or nomads, but to *embrace the identity that accompanies the inheritance*. In this instance, the Danites were to become landowners, farmers, and fishermen – enjoying the riches found within their given portion.

In what ways do gay-identified Christians echo the hill-dwelling Danites?

What do you see when you consider your short-term or medium-term future?

- A fearsome enemy with chariots and weapons?
- A productive and satisfying new venture offering all sorts of possibilities?
- Something else? What would that "something else" look like?

Wrong focus

I don't, for an instance, believe that Christians seeking orientational change from homosexual to heterosexual are the incarnation of the judge Samson! As far as I am concerned, unlike Samson they are not carnal Christians flirting with and accommodating the enemy. If I could think of another way to stimulate your thinking regarding the area of orientational change, I would.

What I want to offer for consideration is one's goal. Set apart by God, Samson knew who he was and that he had been given the role of judge in that region. What we see in this man, however, is someone who does not seek God's chosen way, but uses what he has been given to follow his own determined path.

My questions are:

- Who or what is your point of focus?
- What do you believe are your needs, and how do they differ from your wants?
- In what areas are you less sure that your life priorities are directed by God?

What if?

But what if this tribe had taken God at His word in the first place? What if their response had been like Caleb who, because he believed God's promise, eagerly took on the giant-sized Anakites in the hill country of Hebron? When faced with a seemingly insurmountable problem I always remind myself of Paul's assessment of Abraham back in Romans 4:17–22.

> As it is written: "I have made you a father of many nations." He is our father in the sight of God, in whom he believed – the God who gives life to the dead and calls into being things that were not. Against all hope, Abraham in hope believed and so became the father of many nations, just as it had been said to him, "So shall your offspring be." Without weakening in his faith, he faced the fact that his body was as good as dead – since he was about a hundred years old – and that Sarah's womb was also dead. Yet he did not waver through unbelief regarding the promise of God, but was strengthened in his faith and gave glory to God, being fully persuaded that God had power to do what he had promised. This is why "it was credited to him as righteousness."

From that Scripture I take three helpful points:

- **<u>Recognize</u> genuine difficulties in the situation.** Abraham didn't gloss over the truth of his position. He accepted that, in the natural, this promise of becoming the "father of many nations" seemed unlikely.

- **<u>Trust</u> God as being greater than those.** Abraham's faith in God was greater than his own personal understanding of this situation.

- **<u>Refocus</u> faithfully on the One who is trustworthy.** Abraham did not dwell on the difficulties, such as the age and likely infertility of himself and his wife, but he continued to worship the Lord wholeheartedly. Abraham's response not only glorified God, but also increased his own faith in the One who promises and fulfils (Numbers 23:19).

What if we took God's promises to heart and acted upon them? What if, irrespective of our current situation, we chose to leave the "foothills of fear" and step out into the "rich fertile plains" of our inheritance? What would we need to do?

Peace

Peace is not created by a change in orientation. Peace isn't created by a change in behaviour or attraction. Lasting peace is found in Christ alone, for He *is* our peace. Even if, through counselling and prayer, people succeed in addressing their tendency towards emotional dependency, they are still not guaranteed peace in the core of their being.

There will undoubtedly be a sense of relief and a certain joy that they are now equipped with understanding and a "tool kit" to keep this rather large problem at bay. But those tools may not be of use when issues around attachment or past sexual abuse are being addressed. It is easy to become anxious when faced with yet more challenges. It is only by standing where Christ stood on earth, in the framework of truth − loving the Lord with our whole heart, mind, soul, and strength − that anyone is able to stand in a position of peace. Jesus said this to His disciples:

> I have told you these things, so that in Me you may have [perfect] peace and confidence. In the world you have tribulation and trials and distress and frustration; but be of good cheer [take courage; be confident, certain, undaunted]! For I have overcome the world. [I have deprived it of power to harm you and have conquered it for you.]
>
> John 16:33, AMP

The main reason many of the Danites remained in the foothills was that they were paralysed by fear. Instead of reminding each other of the many times God had provided for them during their wilderness wandering, the tribe chose to focus on the enemy. Instead of looking to Him and believing in His ability, the people chose to concentrate on the challenges and difficulties ahead. Consequently, their faulty focus drained them of all faith.

In the presence of my foes

Taking note of Abraham's three-point plan I mentioned earlier − *recognize, trust, refocus* − we can face the reality of our current struggles. Standing in the security of the framework of truth, we are able to look around at the tribulations, trials, distress, and frustration that Jesus refers to in John 16 during His last session after the Last Supper with His disciples.

269

David likewise was no stranger to such difficulties. Anointed at an early age to be king, David spent the next fifteen years living in hiding, dodging the arrows and spears of jealous King Saul. It was a further seven years before David became king of Israel in addition to Judah and was finally able to rule a united nation. Bearing this in mind, it is worth being reminded of the psalm David wrote while, quite literally, living in fear of his life. David found peace in the midst of his numerous difficulties.

The Lord is my shepherd, I lack nothing.
He makes me lie down in green pastures,
he leads me beside quiet waters,
he refreshes my soul.

He guides me along the right paths
for his name's sake.

Even though I walk
through the darkest valley,
I will fear no evil,
for you are with me;
your rod and your staff,
they comfort me.

You prepare a table before me
in the presence of my enemies.

You anoint my head with oil;
my cup overflows.

Surely your goodness and love will follow me all
the days of my life,
and I will dwell in the house of the Lord
forever.

Psalm 23

Is that your experience? Do you live in the reality of that psalm?

Joshua led the Hebrews into the land of Canaan. Even though the Promised Land was God's land, it was not heaven. There were enemies to engage and conquer. There was land to possess and utilize. There were towns to build and borders to protect. God may well have had His eyes continually upon it "from the beginning of the year to its end" (Deuteronomy 11:12), but it was not a life for the faint-hearted. And neither, in case you hadn't noticed, is the life of a Christian! Thankfully, however, God does not leave us to fend for ourselves.

"You prepare a table before me in the presence of my enemies." Have you availed yourself of the blessings God bestows upon you in your personal Promised Land? Many men and women treat God's provision more like a fast-food drive-through rather than a sumptuous meal to be savoured.

Yes, as we read in Psalm 23, the table is set in full view of everything and everyone – real, perceived, or demonic – but it is there we find God's presence and provision. The choice we have is to sit down at our allocated table setting, or give wide berth to the banqueting table and try to survive using our own resources. The first option builds our faith in spiritual truth and the second option merely reinforces our flawed faith in the physical world.

Once bitten, twice shy?

Have you travelled this way before? Perhaps in the past you have got as far as sitting yourself down, intent on letting God refresh and renew you. Then, before a nourishing morsel has reached your lips, your focus shifts beyond the sumptuously laden table and rests on the face of the enemy. At which point the moment of feasting is past. The enemy manifests in many guises and will certainly know your Achilles' heel. A pornographic website, a longing for touch, or a fear of failure will offer a quick snack and spoil your appetite for more substantial fare.

Other men and women have got as far as being seated at the table, read the menu in full, and ordered their banquet – but have not waited for the dishes to be served. They have failed to "taste and see that the Lord is good" (Psalm 34:8). Merely reading the menu and ordering the food will never fill a hungry belly. To sit and eat without getting stress-induced indigestion requires great trust. Being seated at the table with your back to the enemy is to place yourself in a vulnerable position. To face the food and not the enemy requires faith and trust, and brings to life the Scripture 2 Corinthians 12:9: "My grace is sufficient for you, for my power is made perfect in weakness." Remember, too, what Jesus said to His disciples: "I have overcome the world. [I have deprived it of power to harm you and have conquered it for you.]" (John 16:33b).

Because of Christ's victory through His death and subsequent resurrection, we have hope. With the Holy Spirit's presence in us and upon us, we have power to stand (or sit) in the midst of enemy presence. Remember that Abraham could have looked at his circumstances and weakened his faith.

> Yet he did not waver through unbelief regarding the promise of God, but was strengthened in his faith and gave glory to God, being fully persuaded that God had power to do what he had promised. This is why "it was credited to him as righteousness."
>
> **Romans 4:20–22**

Obedience brings intimacy and strength

The encouraging news is that the more we ingest and digest the things of God, the greater our sense of security will be. As we sit feasting in this unlikely setting, we will become less skittish about enemy presence.

Undoubtedly, the deceit of sin and challenges to our faithful obedience to Scripture will be part of our time here on earth. The lure of the world, the desires of our flesh, and the aggravating prod of the evil one to follow his agenda are not going to go away. However, even as a combined force they are incapable of equalling the banqueting delights that God serves up to envision, strengthen, and equip us to live fully and peacefully in the abundance of God's grace.

After all, we read in 1 John 4:4 that He that is in us "is greater than the one who is in the world". Logically then, the more we feast at God's table, the more our ability to receive, retain, and obey the things of God becomes a way of life. And our love for God is best exhibited through action. Jesus says to His disciples:

> Anyone who loves me will obey my teaching. My Father will love them, and we will come to them and make our home with them.
>
> John 14:23

Admittedly, choosing to remain within God's boundaries in the area of sexuality and sexual expression is not easy, but surely the statement above spurs us on to obedience. We know that the Holy Spirit enters us at conversion, but the phrase "make our home with them" promises so much more than mere occupancy.

Over the years, I have often gone to stay with a particular friend and it isn't an exaggeration to say that I treat it like my

273

second home. If I want a drink I make one, and if I want some food I raid the fridge. There is, as my mother used to say, no standing on ceremony. What believer would not want the Father and the Son to, metaphorically speaking, kick off their shoes, draw the curtains, and make themselves at home?

Learning contentment

Happy feelings follow naturally as a direct result of something pleasant that is happening or has happened. They can also occur if we are able to lay aside or forget our troubles for a period of time. But, like building sandcastles on an expanse of sand at low tide, happiness is always limited by external events. The tide will turn and the encroaching water will gradually reduce the play area until it inevitably tears down and washes away the castles and pretty beach art.

Happiness is one thing. Contentment is another matter altogether. Contentment occurs when we can live with the tension created by accepting that something is not quite right and the certainty that it need not be perfect for life to go on. As my friend Brad once shared with me:

Our actions are never quite good enough, and yet at the same time it's enough to be God's. That tension between the imperfect now and the perfect then creates a dynamic tension that drives us forward. Focus on our imperfections and we stall. Focus on our hopes and we stay in neutral and burn out our fuel. But the right tension between clutch and gas and we go.

None of us can determine our future with great clarity, especially when we consider our current situation regarding orientation, attraction, and behavioural choices.

Paul's claim in the book of Philippians can be applied to all those addressing their same-sex attraction:

> I know what it is to be in need, and I know what it is to have plenty. I have learned the secret of being content in any and every situation, whether well fed or hungry, whether living in plenty or in want. I can do all this through him who gives me strength.
>
> **Philippians 4:12–13**

Unlike Bob, whose testimony we read in chapter 13, I do not feel called to celibacy. I have been celibate for the past thirty years and continue in that state – not because I sense a specific calling on my life, but as an act of obedience to God. I am, however, open to the Lord bringing a gentleman into my life to whom I could commit and marry. I am not, however, discontent with my current situation.

Prioritize

Like Bob, I have learned and continue to learn the importance of precedence. To guard fiercely and jealously my relationship with my first love, Jesus, is always a matter of priority. It has taken so much time and effort to get to this place of sitting calmly at the banqueting table, feasting on the goodness of God, that I do not want anything or anyone to jeopardize this hard-fought position.

In truth, I would only consider entering into a relationship with a man if I believed that it would enhance my relationship with the Lord. Would it open doors to experience more of what it means to love and be loved by Him? Would sharing my life with a husband mean that, together, we could know and further God's Kingdom more than we could as individuals?

Is that not the same for every one of us who faithfully keeps our heart and mind fixed on Jesus, *irrespective* of all that befalls us? Times of trial give us the opportunity to know God more intimately. As I allow Him access to those raw, hurting, and fearful areas, He has the opportunity to prove the truth of His written promises.

Intentional living

Whatever you are doing – watching a movie, writing a book, giving a presentation, eating, or sleeping – you have to stay in God's presence. If you feel great loneliness and a deep longing for human contact, you have to be extremely discerning. Ask yourself whether this situation is truly God-given. Because where God wants you to be, God holds you safe and gives you peace, even when there is pain. To live a disciplined life is to live in such a way that you want only to be where God is with you. The great challenge here is faithfulness, which must be lived in the choices of every moment.[65]

I didn't choose to have emotional and physical attraction toward other women. There wasn't some eureka moment when I made a lifestyle choice to be gay above all other options. From my earliest memories I felt different from other little girls and, as I grew up, that sense of difference morphed into gay attraction, behaviour, and eventually identity.

There was nothing positive about growing up in the mid-1970s, believing that you were gay. It was shameful and isolating and frightening. There were no support groups or leaflets or a society to welcome and affirm you in your unchosen position.

65   Henri J. M. Nouwen, *The Inner Voice of Love: A Journey Through Anguish to Freedom*, New York, New York: Image, Doubleday, 1996, p. 23.

But I am not a victim. I may not have chosen all of those thoughts and attractions, but I do have a choice as to what I do with them. As a non-Christian I saw no problem in acting upon all of those inner impulses and would have continued along that trajectory if the Lord had not chosen to invade my space.

Now, like all believers in every walk of life, I have a choice. As Henri Nouwen wrote: "The great challenge here is faithfulness, which must be lived in the choices of every moment."

What kind of Danite are you? I encourage you to be a member of the "What if" branch of the tribe. They are the ones who possess the spirit of that great man from the tribe of Judah, Caleb. Like him, I encourage you to take God at His word, rely on His promises and provision, and continue to take every metre of "land" that is on offer. As Kara said in her testimony back in chapter 11, *"Change happens… one good decision at a time."*

Bringing same-sex attraction under the Lordship of Christ

In this book we have looked at the wood of the cross and the wood of the vine. Now we need to consider the wood of the yoke. The following Scripture has been cited before:

> Come to me, all you who are weary and burdened, and I will give you rest. Take my yoke upon you and learn from me, for I am gentle and humble in heart, and you will find rest for your souls. For my yoke is easy and my burden is light.
>
> Matthew 11:28–30, J. B. PHILLIPS

Are you weary and burdened by your efforts to "go straight"? Do you feel that well-meaning friends and fellow Christians, albeit silently, are placing unreasonable expectations upon your shoulders? Do you find your faith burdensome? Has your faith-filled walk slipped into an unsure shuffle? What are your expectations? Where is your hope?

We have looked at a number of topics during the course of this book. Together they can be seen as key components in the creation of Christ's yoke that He encourages every believer to wear. As non-believers we wore Satan's yoke and were slaves to sin and death. But now, as believers, we are slaves to righteousness and are yoked with Christ Himself. The more we conform to the image of Christ, the more comfortable that yoke will feel and the greater our peace will be.

Gentle and humble in heart

If I do not cultivate a gentle and humble heart, I will always chafe against the yoke of Jesus. The Scripture in Philippians states quite clearly that Jesus laid aside *everything* in order to become *nothing* and live in obedience to the will of God. His call is our call. The yoke that binds us to our Lord is like an arm that is tenderly draped over the shoulder of a loved one. Why would we stray from such love?

Being firmly convinced that God is good at all times and in every situation maintains the lightness of the yoke. We are able to say "no" to the temptation of sin and the attitude of entitlement, if we remain under Love's restraint. And when we feel lonely or in a place of deep loss because of the godly choices we have made, that same yoke reminds us of His presence, His understanding, and His comfort.

As we voluntarily remain under this Love-yoke we are confident that He will guide us in the right direction. We only have to look at Christ's life here on earth to know that it may not always be the easiest of paths, but we can rest assured that it is the best path. And this path isn't for our feet alone, but is often a "pioneer path" created for the benefit of others. Eugene Peterson's *The Message* captures this spirit:

> So don't sit around on your hands! No more dragging your feet! Clear the path for long-distance runners so no one will trip and fall, so no one will step in a hole and sprain an ankle. Help each other out. And run for it!
>
> **Hebrews 12:12–13**

Just as Christ's love for us took Him to the cross, our love for Him draws us to the yoke. We voluntarily put on and remain under His yoke because the enormity of His love compels obedience. After sharing some difficult teaching that resulted in large numbers walking away, Jesus asked His disciples if they, too, were to leave.

> Simon Peter answered him, "Lord, to whom shall we go? You have the words of eternal life."
>
> **John 6:68**

However hard it is to set aside thoughts, attitudes, identities, and behaviours, Jesus is the answer – not only for salvation, but also for our maturation as Christians. We need to be singularly focused in heart and mind in order to remain comfortably under the yoke of righteousness and walk along the path that He has ordained.

When we combine God's Word with faith and obedience, we will experience the Sabbath-rest described in Hebrews 4. Rest isn't to do with an absence of work, but is everything to do with living in accordance with His commands.

Changed from the inside out

The apostle Paul's conversion was no gentle affair. Saul, as he was initially called, was hell-bent on ridding the world of those who had "contaminated" his religion by putting their faith in a Nazarene called Jesus. After engaging in a time of violent "cleansing" in Jerusalem, Saul headed off to Damascus to continue this purge of the Christ-followers. As we know from Scripture, Saul encounters Jesus on his journey and this man of zealous, but ill-placed, faith is never the same again.

In meeting with the Lord and through subsequent revelation Paul, as he was now called, knew that Jesus' life, death, and resurrected life was sufficient atonement for both Jew and Gentile alike. Paul's calling was to take this revolutionary message to the Gentiles and his primary goal, whatever the cost, was to fulfil this high calling in Christ. Paul's curriculum vitae was impressive and he writes to the Philippians:

> I was born a true Jew, I was circumcised on the eighth day, I was a member of the tribe of Benjamin, I was in fact a full-blooded Jew. As far as keeping the Law is concerned I was a Pharisee, and you can judge my enthusiasm for the Jewish faith by my active persecution of the Church. As far as the Law's righteousness is concerned, I don't think anyone could have found fault with me.
>
> Philippians 3:4–6, J. B. PHILLIPS

In addition to his Jewish credentials, Paul also held Roman citizenship, which afforded him certain privileges not given to other Jews. He was brought up in Jerusalem itself and was highly educated even studying under the great teacher Gamaliel. Without doubt Paul could have lived a very comfortable life of academia and influence and, who knows, may have even married and raised a family!

New heart, open hands

But conversion changes everything. At the point of conversion, a person is born again of the Spirit (John 3:6) and discards the inherited father, the father of lies (John 8:44), in favour of God the Creator and Heavenly Father. Conversion is a life-changing and permanent shift in a person's DNA that is sealed by the presence of God's Holy Spirit *for all eternity*. The significance of this power shift altered everything about Paul and he later writes:

> But whatever were gains to me I now consider loss for the sake of Christ. What is more, I consider everything a loss because of the surpassing worth of knowing Christ Jesus my Lord, for whose sake I have lost all things. I consider them garbage that I may gain Christ and be found in him, not having a righteousness of my own that comes from the law, but that which is through faith in Christ – the righteousness that comes from God on the basis of faith. I want to know Christy... .
>
> **Philippians 3:7–10a**

The Greek word *skybalon* is coyly translated as "garbage" or "rubbish" in most Bibles. The true translation is "animal excrement" – and that gives a more accurate sense of Paul's amazing transformation. The things that this world considers important – power, qualifications, influence, wealth, identity, and self-fulfilment – stink and need to be shovelled up and thrown away. Compared to the fullness of life found in Christ, says Paul, they are nothing and mean nothing. Can we view what is so prized in today's society in the same light?

Identity

Our understanding of the word "identity" influences every aspect of our thinking and behaviour. Every believer has been justified before God at conversion, but the sanctification process is not only a one-time event (1Corinthians 6:11) but also a lifelong process before we finally become like Christ.

The apostle Paul had influence in religious and secular circles. He was a faithful member of God's chosen people and he had the freedom of the most powerful nation in the world at that time. And then Saul/Paul encountered Jesus.

> But there's far more to life for us. We're citizens of high heaven! We're waiting the arrival of the Saviour, the Master, Jesus Christ, who will transform our earthy bodies into glorious bodies like his own. He'll make us beautiful and whole with the same powerful skill by which he is putting everything as it should be, under and around him.
>
> Philippians 3:20–21, *The Message*

Paul was blown away by his encounter with Christ. All that he once prized became nothing to him in the light of meeting with his Lord and Saviour. And that enthusiasm to know Jesus more fully only deepened and matured with each passing year. Paul no longer saw God, himself, or the world around him in the same light. Thus, he willingly relinquished all that was not from God or reflected God in his personhood.

We find all kinds of helpful pointers for our Christian maturation scattered throughout his writing, but I want to finish this book with one verse that is applicable to Christians of all ages and maturity. Paul writes this to the Ephesian church and I have divided the verse (Ephesians 4:22) into three succinct parts:

- You were taught with regard to your former way of life, to put off your old self, which is being corrupted by its deceitful desires

- be made new in the attitude of your minds

- put on the new self, created to be like God in true righteousness and holiness.

May the Lord bless you in your endeavours to bring every aspect of your life under the Lordship of Christ, to live in congruence with God's mandates for sexuality, and to enjoy your growing relationship with Him forever.

Bibliography

Jerry Bridges, *The Fruitful Life: The Overflow of God's Love Through You* (NavPress, Colorado Springs, CO, 2006)

Michael L. Brown, *Can You be Gay and Christian?* (Frontline, Charisma House Book Group, 2014)

William P. Campbell, *Turning Controversy in Church Ministry: A Christlike Response to Homosexuality* (Zondervan, Grand Rapids, MI, 2010)

Lisa M. Diamond, *Sexual Fluidity: Understanding Women's Love and Desire* (Harvard University Press, Cambridge, MA, 2008)

Janelle Hallman, *The Heart of Female Same-Sex Attraction* (InterVarsity Press, Downers Grove, IL, 2008)

Wesley Hill, *Washed and Waiting: Reflections on Christian Faithfulness and Homosexuality* (Zondervan, Grand Rapids, MI, 2010)

Wayne Jacobsen, *In Season: Embracing the Father's Process of Fruitfulness* (Trailview Media, Lifestream, Newbury Park, CA, 2011)

Bill Johnson, *Hosting the Presence: Unveiling Heaven's Agenda* (Destiny Image, Shippensburg, PA, 2012)

Bill Johnson, *Strengthen Yourself in the Lord: How to Release the Hidden Power of God in Your Life* (Destiny Image, Shippensburg, PA, 2007)

Andrew Murray, *Abide in Christ* (Wider Publications, LLC, Radford, VA, 2008)

Andrew Murray, *Absolute Surrender* (Start Publishing LLC, e-book, 2013)

Andrew Murray, *Divine Healing* (Importantia Publishing, e-book, 2010)

Beth Moore, *When Godly People Do Ungodly Things: Arming Yourself in the Age of Seduction* (B&H Publishing Group, Nashville, TN, 2002)

Jenell Williams Paris, *The End of Sexual Identity: Why Sex Is Too Important to Define Who We Are* (InterVarsity Press, Downers Grove, IL, 2011)

Derek Prince, *Entering The Presence Of God* (Whitaker House, New Kensington, PA, 2007)

A.W. Tozer, *The Knowledge of the Holy* (The Fig Classic Series, fig-books.com, 2012)

Tom Wright, *Surprised by Hope* (SPCK, London, 2007)

Philip Yancey, *Disappointment with God: Three Questions No One Asks Aloud* (Zondervan, Grand Rapids, MI, 1988)

Philip Yancey, *Vanishing Grace: What ever happened to the good news?* (Hodder & Stoughton, London, 2014)

Philip Yancey, *What's So Amazing About Grace?* (Zondervan, Grand Rapids, MI, 1997)

Mark A. Yarhouse, *Understanding Sexual Identity: A Resource for Youth Ministry* (Zondervan, Grand Rapids, MI, 2013)

Useful Contacts

Below are points of contact that may assist you in finding more localized help during your journey:

Exodus Global Alliance

Based in Canada, Exodus Global Alliance is a good first step in helping locate a ministry in a person's continent and country.
www.exodusglobalalliance.org

Europe

Live in Christ

Live in Christ (LINC) is an interdenominational association of Christian ministries in Europe.
www.liveinchrist.eu

United Kingdom

Jeanette Howard has no hesitation in recommending both of the ministries below.

Living Out

Living Out is a relatively young organisation created by three Christian leaders who have experienced same-sex attraction. Their website offers testimony, teaching, and advice to those who not only walk a similar path, but also to those leaders seeking to walk alongside the SSA within their own church environment.
www.livingout.org

True Freedom Trust

TFT is one of the oldest ministries in the world that ministers to men and women seeking to address their unwanted same-sex attraction in the light of biblical truth. They oversee small satellite groups around the country and host a yearly conference.
www.truefreedomtrust.co.uk

United States of America

There are two networks in the US that are able to help someone find a recommended ministry. Both networks uphold the traditional biblical belief that sexual expression is best expressed within heterosexual marriage, but they do differ in emphasis as to how that truth is conveyed.

Hope For Wholeness Network

HFWN does not engage in political or cultural dialogue, but offers a pastoral heart to the individual who wants to address their personal, family, or church's response to the subject of homosexuality. They can direct people to the nearest affiliated ministry.

www.hopeforwholeness.org

Restored Hope Network

RHN also recommends ministries around the US that are affiliated to their network. They see their role as engaging in and challenging the unbiblical stance adopted and celebrated in today's society.

www.restoredhopenetwork.com

Australia and the Pacific

Renew Ministries

Renew Ministries has a network of ministries throughout Australia, New Zealand, and the Pacific. Each member ministry will offer their own kind of support to an individual and church body. For more information:

http://www.renewministries.com.au/

Bethany Life
MINISTRIES

Helping Believers Choose The Better Way

www.bethanylifeministries.org.uk

Jeanette Howard is the Director of Bethany Life Ministries. The ministry's focus is to encourage believers to mature into true disciples so that they can stand firm in their faith irrespective of any challenges they may encounter.

BLM is primarily a teaching ministry and Jeanette has spoken at numerous conferences, church retreats, and weekend seminars all over the world. Although these speaking engagements have often been directed to those who have an interest in knowing more about the subject of homosexuality and the Christian faith, her teachings are easily adapted to include everyone who seeks to make Jesus not only their Saviour but also their Lord.

If you are interested in inviting Jeanette to speak then please email: **office@bethanylifeministries.org.uk**

You can keep up to date with the ministry activities and Jeanette's blog via the Facebook page: **https://www.facebook.com/bethanylifeministriesorg**

Our vision is for men and women to know what it is to be rooted and established in Christ, and from that confident position to explore some of the reasons that may have engendered same-sex attraction and homosexual behaviour. Such diligence will result in an intimate life with Jesus and produce quality long-lasting fruit.

(Scripture refs: Ephesians 3:17, John 15:16)